THE TWENTIETH CENTURY

WHAT REALLY HAPPENED

By
Steve Barlow and Steve Skidmore

Illustrated By Roger Langridge

Kingfisher

Kingfisher
An imprint of Larousse plc
Elsley House
24-30 Great Titchfield Street
London W1P 7AD

Copyright © Larousse plc 1996
Text copy copyright © Steve Barlow and Steve Skidmore

First published by Larousse plc 1996

10 9 8 7 6 5 4 3 2 1

All rights reserved. No part of this publication may be reproduced, stored in a retrieval system or transmitted by any means electronic, mechanical, photocopying or otherwise, without the prior permission of the publisher.

A CIP catalogue record for this book is available from the British Library

ISBN 0 7534 0023 5

Steve Barlow and Steve Skidmore have asserted their moral right to be identified as authors of the work in accordance with the Copyright, Designs and Patents Act, 1988.

Designed by Val Carless

Printed in the United Kingdom

CONTENTS

Introduction	5
What was invented? 1900-1918	6
Off to war	7
Travellers' tales	13
World War 1	17
Rights and revolutions	30
The 1920s and 1930s	41
What was invented? 1918-1939	54
World War 2	55
Independence	71
The Cold War	81
Boom!	91
What was invented? 1940-1999	100
Continuing conflicts	102
The end of the century	112
Timeline	120
Answers to quizzes	124
Index	125

INTRODUCTION

The 20th century has sometimes been called the century of the Common Man. We'll call him Joe Soap.

(You can't get more common than that.)

Because of improved education and advances in communications, ordinary people like this have become more aware of what's going on around the world. They have made themselves heard and had more chance to influence the course of events. Sometimes they have been involved in things, like wars, that they would rather have known nothing about.

To find out how ordinary people like Joe and his relatives worldwide made out in this

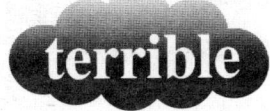

and

century, read on.

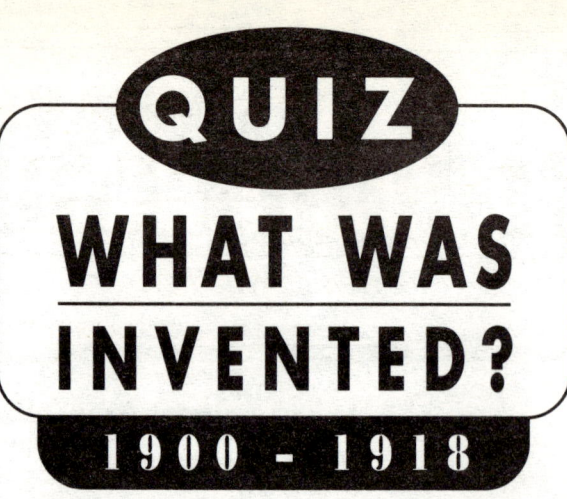

QUIZ
WHAT WAS INVENTED?
1900 - 1918

1. Invented in the first year of the century by Norwegian Johann Vaaler and used for keeping sheets together. There are millions of them, so how is it you can never find one when you need it?

2. Invented by King Camp Gillette in 1901, a device that helped Joe Soap not to slit his throat.

3. The first of these machines, developed by Hubert Booth in 1901, was so big that it had to be pulled along by a horse. A lightweight version was produced by Murray Spangler in 1908. It sucked, but that's okay. It was supposed to.

4. A method, designed by Henry Ford in 1904, of cutting down the time needed to build a car from 12 hours to one and a half hours. (It also introduced the idea of mind-numbingly boring jobs.)

5. Introduced in 1909 by the General Electric Company, this does only one thing; but it does it very well, and in most homes, breakfast just wouldn't be the same without it.

6. You could keep your ear glued to Dunwoody and Pickard's 1910 invention; but if you dropped it, would it shatter into pieces?

7. Developed by Elmer Sperry in 1913, he flies aeroplanes. He's not the pilot or the co-pilot, but you can call him "George".

8. It took nearly 60 years for G.C. Biedler's 1903 invention to become standard equipment in offices. Did it ask pieces of paper to say "cheese"?

9. A hot idea for preserving food? Quite the reverse! This brainwave occurred to Clarence Birdseye in 1917.

(Answers on page 124)

OFF TO WAR

"The sun never sets upon the British Empire," it was said. Why not?

Not because it never got dark in 1900, but because the Empire consisted of colonies all round the world – and so the sun was always shining somewhere that the British had bought, stolen or conquered.

Most wars in the first third of the 20th century were about who owned various colonies. Britain and other European powers had colonies around the world which provided them with *loadsadosh*. It rarely occurred to anyone that these lands really belonged to the people living there. Labour was cheap in the colonies. Profitable crops such as tea and cotton, which wouldn't grow in Europe, could be cultivated there, and many colonies had minerals that didn't occur widely in Europe – especially *gold*. It was gold that led to . . .

7

THE BOER WOER
(that is, the Boer War)

The Boers, or Afrikaners, were mostly descendants of Dutch farmers who first settled near the Cape of Good Hope (South Africa) in 1652. The British then pushed them out of this land and they trekked north, fighting the British on the one hand and the Africans whose lands they were moving onto on the other. Britain took over South Africa and the Boers formed two republics, the Orange Free State and the Transvaal, on land the British thought was worthless.

Then *gold* was discovered in the Transvaal. The Boers, including Joe Van Der Soap, weren't interested (they were farmers, not

miners), but other people were: British "Uitlanders" (immigrants) started to mine the gold and then to take over the Transvaal. In 1899, the Boer republics declared war on Britain. To begin with, the Boers were very successful. They defeated the British three times in a week and, in January 1900, killed 1,200 British soldiers at the Battle of Spion Kop.

They besieged the British for months in **Mafeking**, **Ladysmith** and **Kimberley**. The Brits held

Kop ends
Parts of several football grounds are named after the Battle of Spion Kop. Most famous is the Kop end at Liverpool F.C.'s Anfield stadium, which every other Saturday gets covered by yelling Scousers, empty lager cans and pies that someone's trodden on. It's probably a great comfort to the ghosts of those killed at Spion Kop to know their death is so commemorated. Or possibly not.

> **Boy Scout To The Rescue**
> How did the first Boy Scout help win the Boer War for the British, after all? The defence of Mafeking, which was relieved in May 1900, was led by Colonel Robert Baden-Powell. When he got back to Britain, he took to wearing shorts and in 1908 started the Boy Sprout movement, based on his experiences in South Africa.

The relief of Ladysmith

The news of the **relief** of Mafeking, Ladysmith and Kimberley was greeted with joy all over Britain. Brass bands played, factory hooters hooted, and people came out to dance in the streets. Such excited behaviour is sometimes called "mafficking".

Why such rejoicing? Until this point, the British army had been getting well stuffed. The armies were uneven:
British army: 450,000 soldiers
Boer army: 80,000 soldiers.
With so many soldiers, it should have been a total walkover for the British. But it wasn't.

The war ended with the Peace of Vereeniging in 1902. Part of the treaty was to allow the Boers to continue to deny the vote to Africans in their republics. So the seeds of APARTHEID were already sown. Two other things about the war would appear again:

GUERILLA WARFARE

The Boers were outnumbered, but knew the country where they were fighting much better than the British. So, instead of marching about in the open and waiting to be shot at, they made lightning raids from hiding, then disappeared before the British knew what had hit them. This tactic - known as guerilla warfare - proved so effective that at one point practically every trained British soldier was shipped out to South Africa to try to beat the Boers. In other wars since, most notably in Vietnam, guerilla tactics have proved highly effective. Great numbers of soldiers have been called up to fight the guerilas.

CONCENTRATION CAMP

Ask people, "Who started Concentration Camps?" and they'll probably say "Hitler". In fact, Hitler didn't need to invent these terrible places, because they'd already been invented - by the British. At one time there were nearly 100,000 Boer prisoners in the British camps. Few were Boer guerilas, because the British weren't good a t catching them. Most were women and children from farms the British had destroyed. One third of the people sent to the camps never came out alive.

Mean Medicine

Tea made from goat's dung was tried as a cure for measles in some camps. (It failed.)

THE RUSSO-JAPANESE WAR

Britain, France, Russia, Germany and Italy were the main colonial powers at the beginning of the century. The USA and Japan both wanted to follow suit.

In 1904, both Russia and Japan wanted to take over Korea and Manchuria (part of China). War between them began on February 8, when the Japanese suddenly destroyed the Russian fleet, which was at anchor at Port Arthur in Korea.

News of this disaster arrived in St Petersburg while the Russian Czar was at the opera. So as not to spoil his enjoyment of the evening, officials waited until the end of the performance before telling him about the destruction of half his fleet. *Aaaah!*

Another Russian fleet then set sail from the Baltic and, on its way to Korea - *SHOCK, HORROR!* - attacked and sank a British fleet consisting of **two fishing boats from Hull**. The Russians claimed to have mistaken the trawlers for torpedo boats. What they thought Japanese torpedo boats were doing in the North Sea is hard to imagine. As it turned out, the sinking of the trawlers was the last successful action the Russian fleet managed to carry out.

Battle of Tsushima, 1905

This was one of the greatest naval battles ever fought. Admiral Togo's Japanese fleet surprised the Russians as they came out of a fog bank. 35 of Russia's 38 ships were sunk, disabled or captured. Nearly 5,000 Russian sailors were killed. Japan lost three torpedo boats and 117 men.

It had taken the Russian fleet eight months to sail halfway round the world. It was wiped out in less than twelve hours. For the first time in modern history, an Asian power had defeated a European one.

Signs of things to come

- The Japanese began the war by making a surprise attack on a fleet at anchor. They would do this again at Pearl Harbor during World War 2.

- Russia was utterly humiliated. With thousands killed in battles on land and at sea, the Army and Navy had had enough. The mutiny aboard the battleship *Potemkin* on January 9, 1905, was a key event leading to the overthrow of the Czar in the Russian Revolution.

TRAVELLERS' TALES

By the beginning of the 20th century, most of the world's land had been pretty well explored. Only a few remote tribes in South America were lucky enough not to have had contact with Europeans. Where was left for intrepid discoverers?

A CHILLING STORY

Even though everyone knew that a man with a white beard, a red suit and lots of reindeer had lived at the North Pole for years, people were obsessed with the idea of being first to reach the ends of the Earth. When **Frederick Albert Cook**, an American physician and explorer, claimed to have reached the North Pole on April 21, 1908, the world gasped with admiration:

However, Cook was soon found out to be a cheat and a liar. He told big fibs about his expedition. Not only did he not mention meeting Father Christmas; he also exaggerated how many miles he had travelled.

Cook later claimed to have been the first to climb Mount McKinley in Alaska. This was a lie, too. In 1925, he was convicted of mail fraud. He obviously had trouble spelling his name correctly; it should have been "Crook"!

MEANWHILE, IN CALIFORNIA

(as described in a letter written by our Great Uncle Joseph P. Soapenheimer, when he was still a boy)

Kittyhawk, North Carolina
1903

Dear All

Me and the boys had been joshing Orville and Wilbur about what they call their "hairyplane", shouting things like "Get off and milk it" and "It'll never get off the ground!" None of us believed that they'd get the thing to fly. They're just a couple of guys who make bicycles for a living, for Pete's sake!

They built a rail for the machine to run on (It doesn't have any wheels). But when they tried it, it just dropped off the end of the rail and got stuck in the sand while all the boys haw-hawed. Still Orb and Wilb didn't make no never-mind. They just hauled it out and fixed it and set out for another go.

There were five of us watching (some of the boys had gone home after the first try) when that old hairyplane just lifted off its rails and flew as smooth as silk for maybe 500 feet while we just stood there with our mouths open.

To show it was no fluke, they did three more flights; the best one must have been half a mile, and now I've started saving up to buy a hairyplane of my own...

Another American, **Robert Peary**, had made attempts to reach the North Pole in 1895, 1902 and 1905. In 1909 he tried again, accompanied by Inuit guides and Matthew Henson, his companion on earlier expeditions. This time they reached the pole on April 6. However, before Peary got back, Cook had made his false claim.

When it was shown that Cook had lied about reaching the pole, people began to doubt Peary's story too. He claimed to have covered about 60 km a day on eight days of his journey - which was possible, but barely. For years arguments raged, but in 1989 a new study of his notes and journals showed that it was likely that he had done what he said, and he is now generally accepted as the first to have reached the North Pole.

THE RACE TO THE SOUTH POLE

Captain **Robert Falcon Scott** led his first expedition to Antarctica in 1900-04. He mapped areas that had not been explored before and carried out scientific investigations, but was forced to turn back just a few miles from the South Pole. In 1910 he set off for the pole again, with a team of twelve. He had chosen to use motor sledges but these broke down and this plus bad weather forced seven of the party to turn back in December 1911. The rest pressed on and reached the pole on January 18, 1912, only to find that a Norwegian party led by Roald Amundsen had got there first, a month earlier.

First beyond doubt

The first men proved beyond doubt to have reached the North Pole were four Soviet explorers, Geordiyenko, Sen'ko, Somov and Ostrekin, on April 23, 1948.

IN THE NEWS

26 July 1909

CALAIS-DOVER BY AIR

Frenchman Louis Blériot made the first ever flight across the English Channel yesterday, in a 24 horse-power monoplane.

December 1912

WHY AMUNDSEN GOT THERE FIRST

Some of the reasons why Amundsen beat Scott to the South Pole are:

1) He chose a shorter, overland route.

2) Scott's ship, the *Discovery*, was delayed by sea ice.

3) He used dogs, not motor sledges as Scott did. The dogs were more reliable at pulling the expedition's sleds.

..... and, what's more, Amundsen's party could eat the dogs on the way back. You can't eat a tractor.

The point about the dogs may sound cruel, but the fact is that all Amundsen's men returned safely. None of Scott's group did. First one died after a fall on a glacier. Then Titus Oates, crippled with sickness and frostbite, begged to be left behind to give the others a chance. Eventually, he walked out of the tent into a blizzard saying, "I am just going outside and may be some time". Scott and his remaining companions were eventually found dead only 18 km from the supply depot. Scott was carrying the note that Amundsen had left for him at the South Pole.

First solo journey

Norwegian Erling Kagge reached the South Pole alone in 1993.

WORLD WAR 1

This World War is also known as the Great War.

TRY THESE REASONS FOR SIZE:

🔸 Nearly all the Royal Families of Europe in 1914 were related and, well, you know how families are.

🔸 All the European powers wanted their own big empire. The problem was that, once all the countries of, say, Africa had been taken, the only way of making your empire bigger was to nick a bit of somebody else's.

🔸 All over Europe, people were beginning to demand their rights - sometimes by means of strikes and riots. Russia had already had one revolution. A war (governments thought) would take everyone's mind off their grievances.

🔸 A depressingly childish reason was that the European powers had been busy making new weapons and couldn't wait to try them out.

THE GOOD ASSASSINATION GUIDE

It looks as if Bumping off the Rich and Famous was a popular sport in the early years of the 20th century.

YEAR	NAME	POSITION	CAUSE OF DEATH
1900	Umberto 1	King of Italy	Shot at a gymnastics display.
1901	William McKinley	US President	Shot while opening an exhibition.
1903	Alexander and Draga	King and Queen of Serbia	Shot while hiding in a cupboard.
1905	Grand Duke Sergei	Cousin of Russian Czar	Blown to bits by bomb filled with nails thrown into his lap.
1909	Prince Ito	Japanese Governor	Shot by Korean nationalist.
1911	Peter Stolypin	Prime Minister of Russia	Shot at the Kiev Opera (having survived a bomb in 1906).
1913	George 1	King of Greece	Shot through heart while out walking.
1914	Franz Ferdinand	Austrian Archduke	Shot on motor tour.

The EXCUSE for starting World War 1 was the assassination in June 1914 of Archduke Franz Ferdinand, the heir to the Austro-Hungarian throne, and his wife while they were on a motor tour in Sarajevo in Serbia. The Austrian government used this as an excuse to justify taking over Serbia.

All the main European governments were caught with their trousers down. The German Kaiser was on a yachting holiday in Norway. The head of the German Army was abroad. The French President was in Russia. And the Serbian President was out kissing babies because there was an election coming up.

TIMETABLE TO WAR, 1914

June 28 Assassination of Archduke Franz Ferdinand and his wife in Serbia.

July 26 The Czar warns Austria not to invade Serbia.

July 27 Austria invades Serbia.

July 29 The Czar mobilizes his army.

August 1 The German Kaiser declares war on his cousin, the Czar.

August 3 Germany declares war on France. Britain warns Germany not to invade Belgium.

August 4 Germany invades Belgium.

It would have been easy to stop the war happening, but nobody really wanted to.

WORLD WAR 1:

THE TEAMS

GROUP A:	GROUP B:	GROUP C:	GROUP D:
The Allies	**Central Powers**	**Spectators**	**Neutrals**
Britain	Germany	Turkey	Spain
France	Austria-Hungary	Italy	Portugal
Russia			Holland
			Scandinavia

"What do you think of these line-ups, Jimmy?"

"Well, Des, strong line-ups in Groups A and B mean we could be in for a dour midfield struggle, neither side giving much away. Group C will try to stay out of it, but it's my guess Turkey will be putting the boot in before long."

"And what about the rest of the world? Trevor?"

"Well, Des, once the whistle goes, the ANZACs..."

"Anzacs, Trev?"

"Sorry, Des, bit technical there...Australia and New Zealand Army Corps.... My guess is they'll come in on the side of Britain. Then we'll see quite a bit of fighting down the Gulf End and the Eastern side of the ground."

"I don't think the African nations will be able to stay out of it either, Des: a lot of old scores to be settled there..."

"Thanks, Gary. Well, the news from the stadium is that the play has got completely bogged down in a sea of mud. Neither side is able to move an inch."

"Well, the ref should have called it off, Des. I mean nobody can play in these conditions, the whole thing's a mockery..."

THE terrible TRENCHES

The Generals started off trying to fight "by the Book". The problem was that the Book had been written in the days of single-shot muskets, when soldiers wore bright-coloured uniforms and marched to battle in nice squares. It also had a lot to say about cavalry tactics. Lancers, for example, would charge just like Sir Lancelot. In the first months of the war, armies manoeuvred between the Belgian border and Paris, but by 1916 all that had changed. Both sides had dug defensive trenches, separated by miles of barbed wire and mines. Between the armies lay **"no man's land"**.

The Generals were in trouble. The Book didn't say anything about trenches. What it said was that in an attack Private Joe Soap and his fellow soldiers must:
- carry all their kit
- walk forward at a steady pace in neat rows
- use their bayonets to stab the enemy.

Unfortunately, this didn't work any more. Carrying their kit made soldiers so heavy that they sank in the mud, or couldn't climb over the barbed wire. Joe and his comrades walked into a hail of machine gun bullets. They rarely got close enough to use their bayonets. In following the Book, the Generals sacrificed hundreds of thousands of Joe Soaps, Joseph Savons, Josef Seifes, and so on, for the gain of a few hundred metres of mud.

The trenches were on the Western Front. Conditions in them were appalling. Cold and disease crippled whole armies. Anyone who strayed off the wooden walkways could be sucked to a horrible death in the mud. So, for poor Joe and his fellows, the situation was quite dangerous enough even before they started fighting.

Somme joke, surely?

At the end of the first day of the Battle of the Somme (July 1, 1916), the British Commander-in-Chief, General Haig, said that it had been a good day's work and the position was favourable. But it was surely not so favourable for the 57,000 British dead and wounded. Many of these had been killed in the first thirty minutes.

BATTLES ON THE WESTERN FRONT

Among the greatest battles of the war were:

BATTLE	CASUALTIES
The Marne (1914)	250,000 combined British and French
Ypres (1915)	300,000 British 9,000 French 260,000 German
Verdun (1916)	542,000 French 434,000 German
The Somme (1916)	420,000 British 195,000 French 650,000 German

In 1915 alone, casualty figures were 279,000 British, 1,292,000 French and 612,000 German. In all, over 8 million people on all sides died during the Great War.

FOUR FRONTS

The **Western Front** was where the Central Powers confronted the British, French and Belgians. The **Eastern Front** was where they fought with Russia (whose army was poorly equipped and poorly led).

On the **Balkan Front**, Serbia, Montenegro and Romania (from 1916) fought with the Allies; Bulgaria and Turkey with the Central Powers. Greece was dragged in to join the Allies in June 1917.

When Italy joined the Allied side in April 1915, this produced the **Italian Front**.

The Gallipoli Campaign

In April 1915, the Allies sent an army to fight Turkey. This was a disaster as the army landed on exposed beaches, where there was no shelter from the Turkish guns, and the climate was unhealthy: scorching hot during the day and freezing cold at night. The area was infested with dangerous insects.

The campaign at Gallipoli was abandoned in January 1916. It cost the lives of 252,000 Allied soldiers, many of them from Australia and New Zealand, and the same number of Turkish defenders.

Fighting spread to the African colonies. Japan joined in on the Allied side in August 1914, in order to swipe Germany's possessions in the Far East. In the Middle East, Lawrence of Arabia (an agent of British military intelligence) led an Arab uprising against the Turks.

THE WAR AT SEA

When the war started, Britannia really did rule the waves. The Germans had been building warships at top speed, to try to match the might of the British Royal Navy; but their ships, though newer, were also fewer. Only one major battle was fought at sea: the Battle of Jutland, off Denmark, in 1916.

The Royal Navy lost 3 battle cruisers, 3 cruisers, 8 destroyers and 6,784 men. The German Grand Fleet lost 1 battleship, 1 battle cruiser, 4 light cruisers, 5 destroyers and 3,039 men. The result was a draw, but the Germans were convinced that there was no way they could defeat the Royal Navy in battle. The German fleet retreated to harbour and stayed at anchor for the rest of the war, leaving Britain in possession of the surface of the seas. Instead, the Germans concentrated on **submarine warfare**.

How submarines nearly won the war for Germany

By 1917, German submarines had sunk millions of tonnes of British and French merchant shipping. Nearly 1,000 British warships had been sunk by submarine action and ships' crews were refusing to put to sea. This meant that the Allies could no longer get sufficient supplies from the USA to keep fighting.

How submarines helped lose the war for Germany

The USA was determined to stay out of the fighting. However, in 1915 the Cunard liner *Lusitania* was sunk by a German submarine with the loss of 1,400 lives, 128 of them American. From this point, Americans began to take the war seriously. The USA entered on the Allied side in April 1917 and, even though US troops fought no decisive battles, their coming in was enough to give confidence to the Allies and demoralize the Germans, leading to the eventual Allied victory.

The submarine threat was finally countered by merchant ships sailing in convoys, protected by fast warships. German submarines could do nothing against these formations of ships.

THE WAR IN THE AIR

When the war started, aeroplanes were primitive. Pilots were armed with pistols and bombs no bigger than grenades, which they dropped by hand. Development was rapid. "Pusher" aircraft types (with the propeller at the back) were replaced by fighter aircraft with propellers in front. **Problem:** how to attach a machine gun to make the plane a deadly weapon?

WHERE DO YOU FIX THE MACHINE GUN?

In front? (Problem: you were more likely to shoot your own propeller to bits than to destroy the enemy.)

So put metal blades on the prop, to knock the bullets aside. (Problem: the vibration caused by bullets hitting the prop tended to wreck the engine.)

Use an "interrupter" gear (invented by Germany) that stopped the gun firing while the propeller blade was in the way. (Problem: now all pilots had to worry about was their wings coming off in a dive...)

Once these problems were solved, aeroplanes became more effective. In aircraft like the **Fokker Triplane** and the **Sopwith Camel**, successful aces like Manfred von Richthofen, René Fonck and "Mick" Mannock became national heroes.

The Red Baron

After shooting down a British ace, Germany's top air ace, von Richthofen, had his aeroplane painted red and became known as "the Red Baron", though he wasn't a baron at all. He awarded himself little silver cups for shooting down enemy pilots, and would often land beside the crashed plane of his victim to pick up a souvenir! British pilots hated von Richthofen. When told of his death, one said, "I hope he roasted all the way down."

Zeppelins were giant airships named after the German who invented them at the end of the 19th century. Though slow, they could fly so high that combat aircraft and anti-aircraft fire could not reach them. More than a hundred zeppelins carried out bombing raids on British cities in World War 1. This meant that, for the first time, Joe and Josephine Soap living miles from the front found themselves caught up in the fighting.

Zeppelins ceased to be a serious threat when aircraft were developed which could fly high enough to reach them.

NEW SECRET WEAPONS

POISON GAS

Poison gas (chlorine) was used as a weapon for the first time, by the Germans, at the Battle of Ypres in April-May 1915. The use of this

weapon forced all Allied soldiers to carry gas masks.

TANKS

Tanks were also used for the first time in World War 1. "Tank" was actually a code-name for this new British secret weapon, which came on to the scene in 1916.

Though they travelled at only 3 miles per hour and often broke down, tanks terrified the Germans. Four hundred tanks rolled down on them at the Battle of Amiens in August 1918. This "black day of the German Army" signalled the beginning of the end for Germany.

Death by drowning

Soldiers who were gassed usually died from drowning. The poisonous gas caused the lungs to disintegrate and fill with blood. This meant that the person literally drowned in his own blood.

HOW THE WAR ENDED

The Russian Revolution of 1917 (see page 39) brought the war in the East to an end. With the Allies closing in, the German fleet mutinied in October 1918. By November, the German government had collapsed; the Kaiser, faced with the choice of shooting himself or running away, ran away (surprise, surprise!) to Holland.

Peace terms were negotiated between Germany and the Allies and the fighting of the Great War stopped at 11 o'clock in the morning of November 11, 1918.

PEACE TREATY TERMS

- Britain and France took over Germany's African colonies and also Turkey's old empire.

- Germany lost territory to France and Poland.

- The German Army was limited to 100,000 men.

- The German armed forces were allowed:
  no heavy artillery
  a small navy
  no air force

- Germany had to pay for all the damage caused by the war.

- The Austro-Hungarian Empire was dismantled as Czechoslovakia, Yugoslavia and Hungary were granted independence.

- The League of Nations was established, with the aim of preventing further war.

The terms of the peace treaties were intended to make Germany so weak that it could never go to war again. They had the opposite effect; the German people were humiliated, and they wanted revenge. Their anger was so great that, by the 1930s, they allowed a criminal madman to take over their government. In this way, the seeds of the Second World War were planted in the ending of the First.

RIGHTS AND REVOLUTIONS

ALL THE (SUFF)RAGE

At the beginning of the 20th century the common woman, Josephine Soap, stayed at home and cooked, cleaned, washed clothes, had babies . . . that was about all. But some women began to go out to work and, as they became more independent financially, they started to call for the right to vote – the suffrage.

In Britain, in 1900, only men over the age of 21 had the right to vote. In 1901, twenty women's suffrage societies were set up, and in 1903 Emmeline Pankhurst founded the Women's Social and Political Union. Josephine Soaps who joined became known as suffragettes. Some went on hunger strike.

WOMEN WON THE VOTE:

- In 1907 in Finland.
- In 1913 in Norway.
- In 1915 in Denmark.
- In 1917 in Russia.
- In 1918 in Canada.
- In 1918 in Britain.
- In 1920 throughout the USA.

HOW

BRITISH WOMEN WON THE VOTE

1907-10 Suffragettes vandalized property in the hope of gaining publicity for their cause.

1908 Thousands of women took part in demonstrations and processions which grew more and more violent.

1909 Suffragettes, when arrested, began to go on **hunger strikes.** This forced the government to release them. (Later, such hunger strikers were force-fed.)

1913 The **Cat and Mouse Act:** women who became ill on hunger strike could be released and then rearrested when they were better.

1913 **Emily Davison** ran out of the crowd into the path of the King's horse at the Epsom Derby. She was hit by the horse and died some days later.

1914 The outbreak of World War 1 brought an end to violent suffragette activity. Many more women went to work during the war years.

1918 Women aged 30 and over and who lived (or whose husbands lived) in property valued at £5 or more were allowed to vote.

1919 Nancy Astor became the first female MP.

1928 Women over 21 were given the right to vote and so became equal with men.

COMMON MEN AND WOMEN UNITE!

It wasn't only women who demanded their rights in the early 20th century. Workers, especially in factories, realized that they deserved more money and better working conditions. They expressed their demands by going on strike. Trade union membership was high. In Russia, workers' councils called **soviets** were set up.

Joe and Josephine Soap began to wonder why the people with the power tended to be only from the aristocracy and the upper classes. Why couldn't they themselves have more say about how their countries should be run, who they should fight, what they should pay to the government and so on? They decided that things ought to change.

REVOLTING!

Two revolutions in the early 20th century were the Boxer Uprising (or Rebellion) and the Russian Revolution. Which kind of boxers rebelled?

THE BOXER UPRISING

Fooled you! Neither picture is right. The truth is that **China** at the beginning of the 20th century was dominated by foreign powers. Britain, France and Germany had exclusive trading rights in Chinese ports, and foreigners ran the Chinese post office and were responsible for customs and excises. Foreign banks, insurance and shipping companies were set up. Foreign gunboats patrolled China's waterways. The Chinese greatly resented all this and, in 1900, a group of rebels decided to rid the country of the "foreign devils". Armed groups of rebels were called the **League of Righteous Harmonious Fists** - and this led the Western press to call them BOXERS.

Secretly encouraged by the Chinese government, the Boxers rampaged through the land, killing foreigners, Christian Chinese and Chinese with any ties to foreigners. The climax came when an international force of British, French, German, Japanese, Russian and US troops entered Beijing (Peking) in August 1900 to lift the siege of the foreign embassies there.

Under the subsequent International Protocol of 1901, China was forced to pay a massive fine as a form of compensation and to agree to the stationing of foreign troops in Beijing and eleven other Chinese cities. This caused great resentment amongst the Chinese that would eventually lead to the overthrow of the Manchu dynasty and the success of the Communist revolution (page 84).

REVOLT SUCCESS 0/10

VOWS

Members of the Righteous Harmonious Fists vowed:
- not to be greedy or disobey existing laws
- to destroy foreigners and corrupt officials

THE RUSSIAN REVOLUTION

The Russian Revolution wasn't just one revolution. It was really made up of three. Millions of common or garden peasants, like Josef Sopoyevski, had been toiling away in Russia for years, so why did they want to revolt now?

Czar almighty

For centuries Russia had been ruled by the Czar, who was in a god-like position. He (or she) was Big Boss, and anyone showing any opposition to this idea was swiftly dealt with by having bits of their body cut off, being killed or imprisoned or generally having their life made miserable.

Josef Sopoyevski and his mates scored a minor success when they (or their leader, Sophia Perovskaya) assassinated Czar Alexander II in 1881, but this turned out to be rather an own goal. The next couple of Czars and their supporters decided to be VERY heavy with anyone who had any silly ideas about changing the Russian way of life (in other words, anyone who didn't want to do exactly what the Czar said).

Then, in 1905, as the country suffered famine and there was widespread anger against the Czar, it looked as if things would change. The great Russian Army and Navy were heavily defeated by the Japanese at the Battle of Tsushima (see page 12) and this increased the social unrest. While the peasants were suffering, Czar Nicholas II and his upper-class friends continued to live in luxury. Ordinary Russians like Josef were brassed off.

A **terrible** joke

The peasants are revolting.
You're not too nice yourself.

Russian Revolution Round 1

On January 22, 1905, a priest, Father George Gapon led a march of workers to Czar Nicholas II's Winter Palace in St Petersburg. They were to ask the Czar for better working and social conditions.

As the protesters approached the palace, Russian troops opened fire on them. Five hundred people were killed, including many women and children. The day became known as Bloody Sunday. The ironic fact was that the Czar wasn't even at the palace at the time.

The killings inflamed the Russian people and led to:
- further strikes and protests
- the assassination of the Czar's cousin Grand Duke Sergei (see page 18)
- the formation of soviets (workers' councils).

In June 1905 came a major turning point. On the 27th, a sailor on board the battleship *Potemkin,* based at the Black Sea port of Odessa, complained about the bad food being served. Annoyed by this lack of culinary appreciation, a First Lieutenant shot dead the unfortunate complainer.

The crew mutinied and threw the commander and many officers overboard. The city of Odessa also mutinied, and so the Czar sent 50,000 troops to the city, where 6,000 people were killed.

This brutality led to a general strike in St Petersburg and the Czar was forced into agreeing to open a parliament - called a **Duma**. However, he limited the power of the Duma to make sure that it wasn't able to **Dumuch**.

Over the next two years, thousands were killed in street fighting in Moscow, and there were general strikes and famine throughout Russia. Revolutionary political groups sprang up. The strongest of these were the **Bolsheviks** – who were the forerunners of the Russian Communist Party. They were led by Leon Trotsky and Vladimir Ilyich Lenin.

The Czar dealt with this by getting tough and forcibly putting down opposition; having many political activists assassinated; and executing others, or sending them to **Siberia**.

Siberia

The Eastern region of Russia was used as a penal colony and place of exile. Winter temperatures there are usually below -18°C. When people came out of exile, they "came in from the cold".

Nonetheless, this Round 1 revolt wasn't a total failure - it forced the Czar to grant some rights to Josef Sopoyevski. More importantly, it set the scene for the Russian Revolution Round 2.

REVOLT SUCCESS 3/10

Is Lenin? No, he's out.

And you thought the last joke was

terrible

Ra Ra Rasputin!

Grigori Yefimovich Rasputin was known to his enemies as **The Mad Monk**. He was a Russian priest who claimed to be a magical healer.

The Czar's son Alexi suffered from haemophilia - a condition which meant that if he cut himself, the blood wouldn't clot and he would continue to bleed. Rasputin supposedly "cured" this condition and thus became a great favourite with the Czar's wife, Alexandra (some people claimed that they became lovers).

Russia went to war with Germany in 1914 and while Czar Nicholas was away at the front, Rasputin, with Alexandra's approval, filled government posts with his own friends. They were incompetent and the Russian population became more and more discontented.

Finally, a group of Russian noblemen decided that enough was enough: they would kill Rasputin. On December 29, 1916, Prince Yussupov invited him to a party.

How to Kill a Mad Monk

Try this

confusing

query

on your parents/teacher/probation officer/local Mad Monk, etc:

Prince Yussupov and his friends did all these things to the Mad Monk Rasputin:

1) fed him with cakes and wine poisoned with cyanide (enough to kill several people)

2) shot him several times

3) clubbed him over the head with an iron bar.

So, how did Rasputin die?

?

(The answer is over the page.)

He drowned. The cyanide seemed to have no effect and shooting Rasputin only made him even more mad: he charged through a locked door. Believing him to be dead, the conspirators pushed Rasputin under the ice of the River Neva. He finally died, not from the bullets, the poison or the beating, but by drowning.

Russian Revolution Round 2

By March 1917 Josef Sopoyevski and co. were more than fed up. Not only had they put up with the Czar and his mate Rasputin, but also they had been fighting in World War 1 for three years and had had the stuffing knocked out of them by the German Army. Food was in short supply and many had grown tired of the war. They held strikes in St Petersburg and strikers and troops clashed violently.

The Duma, deciding that it had better **Dusomething** for once, demanded that Czar Nicholas give up his power, and on March 15 a new government was set up, headed by Prince Georgi Lvov.

Nicholas realized that the game was up and abdicated, but not before trying to give the crown to his brother Michael - who said "Bolsheviks" to that idea. Nicholas and his wife and children were then imprisoned in the town of Ekaterinburg.

The provisional government brought in new wage deals, BUT they wanted to continue the war.

REVOLT SUCCESS: 6 / 10

Russian Revolution Round 3

On the night of November 6-7, 1917, the Bolsheviks seized power in St Petersburg (now called Petrograd) by taking over the government's headquarters in the Winter Palace. They established a soviet government led by Lenin and quickly crushed political opposition.

July 15, 1918

TELEGRAM

From: The Central Committee of the Supreme Soviet, Moscow
To: Commissar Josef Sopoyevski, Ekaterinburg

Comrade, We understand that the ex-Czar has appealed to his cousin King George V of Britain for help. Though the King refused, it is dangerous to allow the ex-Czar to live, especially as the White Russian capitalist traitors may attempt a rescue. You are therefore ordered to execute the Czar and all his family.

July 16, 1918

TELEGRAM

From: Commissar Josef Sopoyevski, Ekaterinburg
To: The Central Committee of the Supreme Soviet, Moscow

Comrade, Your instructions have been carried out to the letter. The ex-Czar and his family have been liquidated, along with their doctor, parlourmaid, cook, valet and dog. Long live the Revolution!

The Bolsheviks ended the war with Germany and put in place Communist economic measures.

REVOLT SUCCESS: 8/10

However, many Russians were NOT happy and another civil war took place between Lenin's **Bolshevik Reds** and the **White Russians**.

THE REDS v THE WHITES

"Interesting draw, Jimmy."

"Yes, Des, and there's no problem with a shirt colour clash. Could be a cracking match as long as the Whites can find each other in the snow!"

"Yes, very funny, Jim. Alan, any thoughts?"

"Well, Des, the Whites have got strong support from the foreign players (Germany, France and Britain). The three foreign player rule will be a real help, but you've got to remember that the Reds are under Leon Trotsky. He's a ruthless manager. The Reds have also got a lot of support and that's important. If the crowd gets behind you in a civil war, you're almost certain to win."

LATE RESULT:

Reds Win! Manager Leon Trotsky is to set up the Union of Soviet Socialist Republics (USSR). "The Lads are over the moon," says jubilant boss Leo.

LATER RESULT:

1927: Reds Manager Ousted! Leon Trotsky who led the Reds to victory in the 1918 season was today sacked by Chairman Joe Stalin.

LATER LATER RESULT:

1991: Reds Relegated! The troubled Communist team has agreed to split up the USSR. Russia and Ukraine are under new management and trying to rebuild teams using the Capitalist style of play.

THE 1920s & 1930s

High hopes? Some hope!

British politicians had promised that soldiers coming home from World War 1 would return to a land fit for heroes. So Joe Soap faced the 1920s full of hope and high expectations.

The "Roaring Twenties" were a time of fun – for some people. It was the decade of the Charleston and the jazz boom. Radio began to bring entertainment into homes, and going to the cinema was an increasingly popular pastime. Transport was developing in the air and on the ground, with cars becoming more commonplace.

However, the world was also entering a period of depression, mass unemployment and civil wars. Two opposing doctrines began to dominate world politics: Fascism and Communism. Such a climate led to the rise of dictators in Russia, Italy, Germany, Spain and China. By the end of the 1930s Joe Soap and his fellows all over the world would find themselves involved in another world war.

UP IN THE AIR

1919
First non-stop crossing of the Atlantic in a bomber plane, by John Alcock and Arthur Brown.

1927
First solo crossing of the Atlantic by Charles Lindbergh in his plane, the "Spirit of St Louis". It took him 33 hours, 39 minutes.

COMMUNISM v FASCISM

Communism

The theory of modern-day Communism was set out by Karl Marx (no relation to Groucho) and Friedrich Engels in the Communist Manifesto of 1848.

The main ideas:
- Everybody should own everything, equally.
- There should be no more classes! (That doesn't mean no more school. Hard luck! It means no more social classes, as in upper, middle and lower.)
- Capitalism should be overthrown. (Nothing to do with big letters! It means that people with loads of money should have it taken away – and is an idea thought up by people who didn't have loads of money to lose.)

Fascism

The term Fascism was first used by Benito Mussolini's party, which ruled Italy from 1922-43.

The main ideas:
- Our army's bigger than yours, so we're going to give you a right good stuffing.
- Our country's the best and to prove it we're going to give you a right good stuffing.
- Rich and powerful people are perfectly entitled to give poor people a right good stuffing.
- There should be only one political party, which is allowed to give everyone a right good stuffing.
- The party should be led by a dictator, who can give anyone who disagrees a right good stuffing!!

Mussolini, "il Duce"

Mussolini formed the first Fascist group in Milan and was supported by landowners and industrialists who feared that Communists might take over Italy. After threatening the government, he was invited to take over the running of Italy in 1922. He called himself "Duce" (leader) and set an example for other would-be Fascist leaders, including Hitler.

TEN THINGS YOU DIDN'T KNOW ABOUT BENITO MUSSOLINI

1. His father was a blacksmith.

2. He started his career as a Socialist.

3. His followers were called Blackshirts.

4. When his followers marched on Rome to seize power, he stayed in Milan ready to hop it to Switzerland if things went badly.

5. He survived an assassination attempt in 1926, when a bullet fired by Violet Gibson, the daughter of an Irish peer, grazed his nose.

6. After this, the Pope declared that Mussolini was protected by God. In return, Mussolini allowed the creation of the Vatican State.

7. Mussolini had the conductor Arturo Toscanini beaten up for refusing to play the Fascist National Anthem.

8. He watched as Italy won the World Cup in 1934. The entire team had given the Fascist salute during the playing of the National Anthem.

9. He used poison gas in his conquest of Ethiopia in 1936.

10. He named Fascism after the Ancient Roman symbol, the Fasces, which was a bundle of sticks with an axe sticking out.

DEPRESSION

The depression of the 1920s and 1930s could not be cured by taking happy pills or seeing a psychiatrist. All over the world governments were hit by rising costs, unemployment and a lot of people who were very naffed off with things in general.

In Britain, soldiers returning from the Western Front expected to find jobs, houses and a better way of life. Instead they came up against social conditions that had barely improved, inflation and cuts in wages. Seriously fed up, Joe Soap and his mates all took part in a General Strike in May 1926 and brought the country to a near stand-still. However, after only nine days the strike failed. This was partly because many upper-class twits, who had always wanted to be engine or bus drivers, took over the striking workers' jobs. Of course they only had to do it for a few days, as most people couldn't afford to stay on strike for longer.

Unemployment continued and in the 1930s hundreds of Joe Soaps went on hunger marches to highlight the plight of the poor.

Crash, bang, wallop!

Even the USA was unable to avoid the economic problems. In the Wall Street Crash of 1929, thousands of people lost money as share prices plummeted (and so did businessmen when they jumped out of the window). Banks went bust as confidence drained out of the fragile economy. Now the depression really set in.

A vicious circle

Person loses Job → No money → Can't buy goods → Factories can't sell goods → Need less workers → (Person loses Job)

By 1933, 13 million Americans were out of work. The new President, Franklin D. Roosevelt, introduced an economic programme called the New Deal and this brought some relief. The government poured money into large-scale building schemes in order to get people back to work. However, it was to take something extraordinary to <u>end</u> the depression - World War 2.

No more alcohol

On January 17, 1920, alcohol was banned in the USA. This prohibition followed years of campaigning by people who thought that alcohol was evil and wasteful. But the actual result was to encourage the illegal manufacture and sale of booze. Soon, gangsters took over the distribution of alcoholic drink, and cities like Chicago became the centre of bloody warfare between gangs led by Al Capone, Frank Yale and Johnny Torrio. Hundreds of people died and corruption became widespread amongst politicians, the police and judges. Prohibition was ended in 1933. Cheers!

GERMANY'S DEPRESSION

At the end of World War 1, Germany had been forced to pay large sums of money to the winning nations and say –"Sorry-for-starting-it-and-we promise-not-to do-it-again". As a result of paying these reparations, Germany was in a financial crisis. Inflation meant that the Mark* became almost worthless, cheaper than wood to burn.

The rise of prices

For Joseph Soapernickel, the price of bread went up and up:

1918	0.63 Marks
1922	163.15 Marks
Jan. 1923	250 Marks
July 1923	3,465 Marks
Sept. 1923	1,512,000 Marks
Nov. 1923	201,000,000,000 Marks!

This hyper-inflation led to great social unrest. People were starving. They couldn't buy goods, and businesses went bust. Unemployment led to anger and violence.

* No relation to Groucho or Karl. It's a unit of currency.

The rise of Hitler

Out of the situation, a new threat emerged - a man called Adolf Hitler, who became the leader of the German Workers' Party in 1921 and renamed it the National Socialist Workers' (Nazi) Party. Nazism was Hitler's own form of Fascism.

In 1933 he became Chancellor of Germany and in 1934 President, calling himself "Führer" (leader). His opponents were crushed and Germany was turned into a war machine to fulfil the Nazi dream of "Ein Reich, Ein Volk, Ein Führer" (one state, one people, one leader).

TEN THINGS YOU DIDN'T KNOW ABOUT ADOLF HITLER

1 He was often beaten by his father.

2 He loved his mother and her death in 1907 was a terrible blow for him.

3 He dropped out of high school and was refused a place at the Academy of Fine Arts in Vienna.

4 After an attempt to seize power ended in Munich in 1923, he was sentenced to 5 years in prison but released after 8 months.

5 His friend Rudolf Hess suggested that he write a book to keep himself busy in jail. Hitler wanted to call it "Four and a Half Years of Struggle Against Lies, Stupidity and Cowardice", but friends told him that was a bit long so he called it "Mein Kampf" (My Struggle) instead.

6 He disbanded the German branch of the Boy Scouts and replaced it with his own Hitler Youth movement.

7 One of his laws said that children could be taken away from parents who refused to bring them up as Nazis.

8 He encouraged production of the Volkswagen Beetle, though he didn't design it, as is sometimes claimed.

9 He created the German Autobahn (motorway) system.

10 He was vegetarian.

THE HOLOCAUST

A key idea of Nazism was that the Germans were a superior race, not to be spoiled by mixing with others. This warped belief led inevitably to the Holocaust.

In "Mein Kampf", Hitler blamed the Jews for everything that had gone wrong in Germany. Persecution of Jews was nothing new; Europe has a long and dishonourable history of telling lies about Jews and then massacring them. But it took the Nazis to invent the "Final Solution" to the Jewish "problem". It made perfect sense, if you were an insane bully with no imagination. All you had to do was kill the Jews. All of them.

Hitler and the Nazis also persecuted and murdered:

- communists
- homosexuals
- gypsies
- the mentally ill
- anyone else who wasn't tall, blue-eyed and golden-haired (like Hitler, presumably).

Nevertheless, Hitler reserved his greatest spite for the Jews. Between 1933 and 1938 the Nazis boycotted Jewish businesses, hounded Jewish doctors, lawyers and teachers, and made marriage between Jews and non-Jews illegal. They also began to set up Concentration Camps.

Kristallnacht ("night of broken glass")

On the night of November 9-10, 1938, following the assassination of a German official by a Polish Jew in Paris, Nazi stormtroopers smashed up Jewish homes, businesses and synagogues and arrested 20,000 people. To add insult to injury, Hitler blamed the damage on the Jews and made them pay a $400 million fine.

The beginning of World War 2 saw Hitler taking steps to eliminate the Jews completely.

Jews killed in World War 2

- After Hitler invaded Poland in September 1939, 3 million Polish Jews were tortured or murdered. Jews were herded into ghettos, parts of a city fenced off from the rest. 700,000 died of disease and starvation during the next two years.

- During the invasion of Russia, 33,771 Jews were machine-gunned on September 29-30, 1941, at Babi Yar near Kiev.

- Jews in their hundreds of thousands were transported to Concentration Camps and murdered by cyanide gas or carbon monoxide gas, electrocution, lethal injections, flamethrowers and hand grenades. The numbers of Jews killed in Concentration Camps were:

    Auschwitz: up to 3 million

    Belsen: over 115,000

    Dachau: over 70,000

    Treblinka: 800,000

By the time the war ended, 6 million Jews, two-thirds of the European population, had been murdered by the Nazis: more than had been killed in the previous 1,900 years of oppression.

NATIONALISTS AND COMMUNISTS IN CHINA

While Fascists came to power in Italy and Germany, Communists tried to gain control in China.

China had long been ruled by foreigners and by the corrupt Manchu dynasty. In a rebellion of 1911, Sun Yat-sen and his Nationalist supporters had overthrown the Manchus and Sun had been claimed president of a new Republic of China. However, Chinese warlords continued to fight for power, and the foreigners were still there. Jao Zo-ping had had enough. In a near riot on May 4, 1919, he and 5,000 students protested against foreign intervention in China, and this led to a new wave of Nationalism. The movement was named, rather obviously, the May the Fourth Movement.

The Chinese Communist Party (CCP) was set up in 1921, with the aid of Russian Communists. Sun Yat-sen's party, the Kuomintang, paired up with the CCP and took advice from the Russians on how to organize the Kuomintang and make it more popular. Then Sun Yat-sen died and the new leader of the Kuomintang, Chiang Kai-shek, finally overthrew the Chinese warlords and established a Nationalist government.

Chiang feared the Communists and so, in April 1927, he ordered a massacre of them in Shanghai. Those who survived set up bases, called "soviets", in the countryside, including the Jiangxi soviet in southeast China. Here a former librarian, Mao Tse-tung, recruited peasants. He had been a leading figure in the May the Fourth Movement and one of the founders of the CCP. He likened the Chinese peasants to the sea, in which the Communists would swim like fish.

In 1931 a new enemy appeared: Japan invaded the Chinese state of Manchuria and set up a puppet government under Pu Yi, the last emperor of China.

The Long March

In 1930-34, Chiang Kai-shek sent out extermination squads to try to defeat the Communists. Mao Tse-tung realized that, in order to survive, the Communists would have to move and so, in October 1934, 90,000 of them set off on a 6,000-mile march to a new base in Shaanxi in the northwest. The march took a year and covered some of the most difficult terrain in China. Over half the marchers didn't survive the terrible conditions. The survivors eventually set up their base at Yanan, and Mao, now head of the CCP, wrote a rule book of how Chinese Communism should progress.

Truce

In July 1937 the Japanese invaded China. The Communists and Nationalists joined forces again, to fight the invaders; but both sides knew that this was only a truce in their own battle to rule China.

RUSSIAN AROUND, 1920s AND 1930s

After the Bolsheviks won the civil war in Russia (page 40), they began to make the country Communist. It wasn't affected by the depression.

In 1924, when Lenin died, Josef Stalin took over as Communist leader and, through a ruthless reign of terror, pushed forward a series of economic "Five Year Plans" with the aim of industrializing Russia. Land was divided up amongst "townies", who had no idea how to farm it. Thousands starved to death and any peasants who objected were dealt with mercilessly. Up to 30 million are thought to have died.

Stalin ruled as a dictator and, from 1935, began a series of purges to get rid of any form of opposition (real or imagined). Thousands of members of the Communist Party and the armed forces were murdered. However, despite Stalin's cruelty, many people in the West saw Russia as a workers' paradise and wished to imitate it by creating Workers' States in their own countries.

ON THE NEWS
Bye Bye, King!
In Britain in 1936, King Edward VIII abdicated. He wanted to marry Wallis Simpson, an American who had been married and divorced twice before. The British government thought that Mrs Simpson was not suitable and, anyway, they didn't want a queen with a man's name. They demanded that either the king should marry someone they approved of or should give up the throne. He chose love and gave up his kingdom and empire! His younger brother became King George VI.

Down from the air
1929 The Graf Zeppelin airship flew round the world.
1930 The British airship R101 crashed into a hill, and burst into flames near Paris. 48 out of 54 crew and passengers died.
1937 The German airship Hindenburg exploded as it tried to land in New Jersey. 34 people died and so did people's enthusiasm for airships.

QUIZ
WHAT WAS INVENTED?
1918 - 1939

1. A sweet discovery for diabetics, made by Canadians Sir Frederick Banting and Dr Charles Best in 1921.

2. At 10 kg, it was big to go on your shoulder or in your pocket; but J. McWilliams Stone's 1922 invention is still a favourite with joggers.

3. Developed in 1926 and perfected by Ernst Ruska in 1933, this powerful scientific instrument made it possible to see viruses.

4. In 1928, German Fritz Pfleumer invented a device for capturing the voice.

5. Also in 1928, Dr Alexander Fleming discovered the value of mould (although his discovery was not mass-produced until 1943).

6. Invented by Percy Shaw in 1933, a safety device named after part of an animal that helps drivers to stay on the road after dark.

7. The owner of the Humpty Dumpty Store in Ohio, USA, introduced these to help shoppers in 1937.

8. Named after its Hungarian inventor, it appeared in 1938. You write with it, but it's not a pencil or a fountain pen.

9. Introduced in the USA in 1938, an item of clothing that women wore and men appreciated. Sheer delight!

10. Built by Russian Igor Sikorsky in 1939, it went straight up – and straight down: into aviation history.

(Answers on page 124)

WORLD WAR 2

At the end of the 1930s:

Germany
- still felt humiliated by the terms of the peace treaty after World War 1 and wanted revenge
- was broke (German money was so worthless that it was cheaper to paper your walls with it than to use it to buy wallpaper)

Italy
- was also in bad shape economically
- wanted an empire

Japan
- had been expecting a reward for fighting on the Allied side in World War 1, and hadn't got it
- wanted more land in the Pacific, at the expense of Britain, the USA and China.

All three countries had turned to dictators to get them out of the mess they were in and win them back their pride.

	ITALY	**GERMANY**	**JAPAN**
LEADER	Mussolini	Hitler	Emperor Hirohito
POLITICS	Fascism	Nazism	Shintoism
IMPERIAL AMBITIONS	North Africa	Eastern Europe	China, the Pacific

Shintoism was a warrior-code which worshipped the Emperor as a god.

THE ROAD TO WAR

Italy, Germany and Japan had all begun to build up huge armies and threaten their neighbours. But the rest of the world seemed to ignore this obvious threat. Why?

- The League of Nations was supposed to keep the peace, but had no power.
- Britain followed the policy of appeasement (negotiating and granting other countries what they asked for, in order to avoid war). This boiled down to letting Hitler and the countries that sided with him do whatever they wanted, as long as they left Britain alone.
- The USA was determined to stay out of European affairs.
- The USSR had its own problems. Millions had died from famine, and the country was in no fit state to fight a war.
- France had built a huge line of fortifications on the border with Germany (the Maginot Line) and thought it was safe from German attack.

COUNTDOWN TO WORLD WAR 2

FIVE: **The Spanish Civil War** (1936-39)
This was a dress-rehearsal for World War 2. Germany and Italy supported the Fascist army of General Franco. Though the USA, Britain and France remained neutral, volunteers from these countries fought on the other, Republican side (which lost).

FOUR: **Italy's invasion of Ethiopia** (1936) **and Albania** (1939)
This provided Mussolini with the empire he'd wanted.

THREE: **Unification of Germany and Austria** (1938)
This united the two Nazi states in a strong alliance.

TWO: **Germany's invasion of Czechoslovakia** (1938)
Britain and France allowed Hitler to get away with this, provided that he promised not to invade anybody else. (Some hopes.)

ONE: **The "Pact of Steel"** (1939)
Signed by Hitler and Mussolini, this created the alliance of Fascist states known as the Axis.

ZERO: **The Invasion of Poland** (1939)
The USSR and Germany invaded Poland on September 30. Stalin and Hitler had agreed to divide the country between them.

Britain and France finally realized that they had to stand up to Hitler and declared war on Germany on September 3, 1939.

WORLD WAR 2:

THE TEAMS

GROUP A:
The Allies

Britain
France

GROUP B:
The Axis

Germany
Austria
Italy

GROUP C:
Spectators

Russia
USA
Japan

GROUP D:
Neutrals

Spain
Switzerland
Sweden

GROUP E:
Commonwealth

Canada
Australia
New Zealand

GROUP F:
Africa

Tunisia
Libya
Egypt

"Bigger competition this time, of course, Jimmy."

"Well, yes, Des. Group B looks very strong. Group A are the holders, of course, but their preparation has been patchy. Group C holds the key to the whole contest. Will they join in, and if so, on which side?"

"I think Group D will manage to stay out of it, Des, but the Commonwealth countries will come in to support Group A. I've got a feeling we could see a lot of early competition in Group F."

"Thanks, Trevor. Well, Poland and Czechoslovakia didn't make the final round; what do you reckon to France's chances, Alan?"

"They've got a good defence, don't give much away at the back, but if they can't make the Offside trap work for them, they could be in trouble . . ."

WORLD WAR 2: CHECKMATE IN 13 MOVES

1 1940: Germany invades Denmark and Norway. Winston Churchill becomes Prime Minister of Britain.

2 1940: Germany invades the Netherlands, Luxembourg and Belgium. By attacking through Belgium, the German Army goes round the back of France's famous Maginot Line of defences, which becomes useless. (Whereas the Kaiser failed to conquer France in 4 years of fighting, Hitler has succeeded in 4 and a half weeks.)

3 1940: **Dunkirk**. The British Expeditionary Force, fighting in France, is pushed back to the Channel and it appears that nothing can save it. BUT . . . a fleet of 850 tiny craft sets sail from England; the Royal Navy is joined by pleasure steamers, private yachts, fishing boats, ferries, almost anything that floats. 338,000 troops are rescued, turning defeat into a strange kind of victory.

4 1940-41: **The Battle of Britain**. Hitler assembles an invasion force to defeat his last enemy, Britain, but first he must destroy the RAF. The aircraft of Germany's Luftwaffe are ordered to bomb British airfields. The RAF shoots down more planes than it loses, but the German air force is bigger. The RAF is on the point of collapse when the Germans change tactics. A British bombing raid on Berlin, though it causes little damage, infuriates Hitler who never thought his capital could be attacked. He orders the Luftwaffe to switch to attacking British cities (the "Blitz") and this gives the RAF time to recover.

5 1940-43: **The Battle of the Atlantic**. Convoys bringing supplies from the USA provide Britain with a lifeline. To start with, Germany has only 26 U-boats (submarines), but these begin to attack. German captains find a successful new tactic: the U-boats hunt in "Wolf-Packs" which can split up a convoy and make it easier to hit. Hundreds of ships and thousands of lives are lost. This longest battle of the war is not won until 1943 when, thanks to new detection devices and aircraft carrying depth-charges, the Allies get the better of the dreaded U-boats.

The Tide Turns:

6 June 1941: **The invasion of the USSR**. Believing that Britain is helpless, Hitler turns on Stalin and invades the USSR. He is so confident of victory that the German troops aren't even equipped for the winter. Big mistake! The fighting is brutal. At the Battle of Stalingrad, 300,000 Germans are killed. During the siege of Leningrad, 1.5 million defenders die, but the German Army is forced to retreat.

7 December 1941: **Japan bombs Pearl Harbor**. Japan's surprise attack on the US fleet in Hawaii sinks 18 US ships and destroys 200 aircraft, for the loss of 29 Japanese planes. Japan captures Hong Kong, Singapore and the Philippines, but the USA now joins the Allied side.

8 June 1942: **The Battle of Midway**. US carrier-based aircraft hammer the Japanese fleet and turn the tide of war in the Pacific.

9 October 1942: **The Battle of El Alamein**. The Afrika Korps, led by German General Rommel, has been sent to help Italy win the war in North Africa. But at El Alamein Allied troops force Rommel's men to turn back from Egypt and retreat into Libya. British General Montgomery and his new US ally, General Eisenhower, capture more than 250,000 German and Italian troops when Tunis falls.

10 September 1943: Italy surrenders and deposes Mussolini, but the invading British and US forces and the German Army continue to battle it out. Mussolini is rescued from jail by German commandos, only to be caught and shot by resistance fighters in 1945 and hung upside-down from the roof of a petrol station in Milan.

11 **D-day**, June 6, 1944: The Allies invade Normandy in "Operation Overlord". The greatest invasion force ever assembled begins the liberation of mainland Europe.

12 May 1945: **The Fall of Berlin and German surrender**. With Allied troops approaching, Nazi commanders have fled Berlin; but Hitler has stayed in his headquarters there, still ordering non-existent armies to come to Germany's defence.

> SEND ZER BRIGADE OF HONEY MONSTERS TO STOP ZER RUSSIAN ADVANCE AND MY FLYING SAUCER TO BOMB LONDON!

However, in April, before the arrival of Soviet troops in Berlin, Hitler has committed suicide, with his lover, Eva Braun.

13 September 1945: **The Defeat of Japan**. The USA retakes island after island in the Pacific, and recaptures the Philippines. British and Commonwealth troops retake Burma, and China pushes back invading Japanese forces. Japan surrenders, after the bombing of **Hiroshima** and **Nagasaki,** on September 2, 1945.

THE COMMON EXPERIENCE

The German tactic of "Blitzkrieg" (Lightning War) meant that ordinary people at home in Britain were all in the front line. The tactic was to bomb whole cities into submission; and then the German Army would roll over the survivors.

Another way in which the war affected families throughout Britain was that food was scarce, especially when U-boats began sinking Atlantic convoys.

The government introduced rationing. To start with, each week everyone was allowed:

> 4 ounces (110 grams) of butter
>
> 12 ounces (330 grams) of sugar
>
> 4 ounces (110 grams) of cooked bacon or ham
>
> 3.5 ounces (95 grams) of uncooked bacon or ham

Death by banana

Bananas were no longer imported to Britain during the war so, by the end, no-one had seen a banana for five years. When they finally reappeared in the shops, a three-year-old girl from Bridlington, Dorothy Shippey, ate four at a go. She died.

The Blackout

So that German bombers wouldn't have any targets to aim at, nobody was allowed to show a light anywhere. It could be

exciting

confusing

and

terrible

- House windows had thick curtains, and people were also told to paint the windows black round the edges.
- Buses had no lights. People therefore ended up sitting on each others' laps and bus conductors complained that passengers were diddling them over fares.
- Car headlights had to be covered so that just a tiny slit let light out. Road accidents doubled until this blackout

---

TOP FASHION TIPS
Fed up of not being able to look tip-top because of rationing? Try these hot tips:

- Use beetroot juice instead of lipstick.

- Paint your legs with gravy browning to make it look as if you're wearing stockings. Don't forget to pencil lines down the back of your legs to make it look as though you've got seams.

- Shorten those skirts. You'll not only get admiring looks from all the men, but also save cloth.

- And all you men can save cloth as well – how about wearing trousers without turnups?

- Yes war is hell, but we've all got to make those sacrifices!

A letter to Joe Soap, British soldier, from his Dad

London, 1940

Dear Joe

I hope this finds you as it leaves us. We miss you but they say it'll all be over by Christmas. Anyway, while you're off fighting with the army, me and your mum are doing our bit for the war effort. I've joined the A.R.P. You get an armband saying "Warden" and a hat. They've also given us:

one hand-operated stirrup pump to put out incendiary bombs, and
one long-handled shovel to scoop sand or dirt over them.

We got some training from the Council. The council bloke showed us a cardboard coffin. He said they had hundreds of them, for when the bombing started. I must say this didn't sound very reassuring. He also said everyone should carry a luggage label with their name and address in case they get killed before identity cards can be issued. Proper little ray of sunshine.

I have to check everyone's carrying their gas mask. Just because Jerry hasn't used gas yet, people get careless. I stopped one woman last week who was using her gas mask case to carry her make-up! How daft can you get? I keep my sandwiches in mine.

If you see Hitler, give him one for me.

Love, Dad.

Sheltering from the bombs

Many British cities, including most major ports, were bombed repeatedly. London suffered the most prolonged bombing campaign, known as the Blitz. The worst night was May 11, 1941, when 1400 people were killed by 440 tonnes of German bombs.

People built and used shelters, outdoors:

and indoors:

Cellars and basements were also used as shelters. Pub cellars were especially popular.

Open for Business

The bombing of London caused chaos, but not everything stopped. A police station in a bombed-out area put a sign outside warning would-be criminals:

"Be good – we're still open!"

In London, Underground railway stations were used as air-raid shelters. People slept, or tried to, on the platforms.

The German bombing on London was **terrible** but, in comparison with the later bombing of German cities by the Allies, it was chickenfeed. The RAF and US Army Air Corps bombed Hamburg in 1943. 10,000 tonnes of bombs were dropped in eight days. 200,000 people were killed.

MIND THE BOMBS. MIND THE BOMBS.

A fateful trip

The worst shelter incident happened, not because of bombing, but because a woman slipped and fell going into the Bethnal Green shelter, and people started piling in on top of her. 178 people were killed in the crush.

The bombs increase

When the RAF bombed Dresden, they created a "Fire Storm". Their incendiary bombs started fires that not only burned all in their path, but also used up all the oxygen in the air. Thousands of people were found untouched by fire, but dead of suffocation. 130,000 people died.

Hitler then launched his new secret weapons on London: the V1 and V2 (Vergeltungswaffe, or Vengeance Weapon) flying bombs.

	Max speed	Propulsion	Casualties caused
V1	645 km/h (400 mph)	Jet	46,000
V2	5,600 km/h (3,500 mph)	Rocket	10,000

The ultimate bombing

Japan finally surrendered when the USA dropped two atom bombs on two Japanese cities in 1945. The single "A"-bomb that was dropped on Hiroshima killed 80,000 Japanese people. The bomb on Nagasaki killed 40,000.

The casualty toll was lower than at either Hamburg or Dresden, but the damage had been caused by only two bombs. And suppose you could put an "A"-bomb on the end of a V2 rocket? Boy, would you have a weapon then!

Evacuation

Before the war, over 13,000 well-off women and children fled from Britain to Canada to be out of danger. The Queen and her daughters (now the Queen Mother, Queen Elizabeth and Princess Margaret) refused to join them. To escape the bombing of British cities, over 1.5 million children were sent away from their families to stay with people in the country where it was safer. They were allowed to take with them only: spare clothing, a toothbrush, a comb, a handkerchief and enough food for the journey. Homesickness drove many of them to return home, just in time to be caught in the Blitz. A second wave of 40,000 evacuees left London in 1944 to escape the threat of V1 and V2 missiles.

Little Wittering Suffolk 1939

Dear Mam

I don't like being vacuated. The people we're staying with are dead snobby. People in the village say we don't wash and we've got head lice. What if we have? Aint our fault. I can't sleep, it's so quiet. When I went out this morning, a great black thing leaned over the fence and roared at me. I screamed the place down. The missus came out and said, silly girl, it's only a cow. How was I supposed to know? I aint never seen one.
I reckon I can't stick it here. I want to come home.

love Minnie Soap (aged 8)

THE COST OF WAR

Over seven times as many people died in World War 2 as in World War 1. Total casualties worldwide were 55 million.

Casualties in some of the countries involved were:

the USSR	21 million	Britain	0.5 million
China	14 million	France	0.5 million
Japan	2 million	Germany	7 million

RESULTS OF THE WAR

- Millions of women had been employed in war industries, doing what had been regarded as men's work. Why shouldn't this continue in peacetime?

(**hopeful!**)

The movement for **women's liberation** was soon to develop very strongly.

- The **United Nations** was established as the world's peace maker.

- The Emperor of Japan was not allowed to be a god anymore.

- Germany was divided into **East** and **West**. Germany would not be reunited for 45 years.

- Britain, the USSR and the USA forgot their differences – until about five minutes after the Armistice; then the USSR fell out with her Western allies. Both sides raced to be the first to be able to knock out the other with "A"-bombs carried by guided missiles. The **Cold War** had begun.

INDEPENDENCE

Between the two World Wars, more people had come to think that countries claimed by the European empires should be given independence. They should be allowed to rule themselves.

The Europeans tended to think that this should happen <u>eventually</u>. The people in the colonies thought it should happen <u>immediately</u>. Not surprising, since the colonists had made local people work hard to grow crops such as tobacco, which they couldn't eat, or to dig up minerals such as coal, for which they had no use – and, in return, had given them diseases, for which they had no cure, and destroyed the traditions which used to give their lives meaning.

Canada, Australia, New Zealand and South Africa, countries of the British Empire to which many white Europeans had moved, had always been allowed more freedom than others. They were called Dominions. Between the wars they were given their independence and became part of the British Commonwealth of Nations.

Another Dominion was the Irish Free State (Eire). However, it left the Commonwealth in 1939.

And there was talk about making India a Dominion, <u>eventually</u> . . .

After World War 2, the movement towards independence gathered speed. The European powers had been weakened by the war, and a general belief in equality had taken hold.

INDIA: THE PEACEFUL REVOLUTION

People in India had started to campaign for independence at the end of the 19th century. After World War 1, the campaign was led by Mohandas Gandhi and Jawaharlal Nehru. The methods of protest they used were non-cooperation and civil disobedience – methods Gandhi had first tried in South Africa. He coined the word **"Satyagraha"** (Sanskrit for "truth and firmness") for this non-violent style of protest.

Satyagraha is easy in some ways. You don't have to fight or do anything active; you simply refuse to do as you're told. In other ways, it's far harder than fighting. If someone threatens to shoot you, you can't thump them; you just have to sit and let them decide whether to shoot or not. So it doesn't take any effort - just incredible amounts of bottle!

When Gandhi led his Satyagraha campaigns in India, the British authorities were stumped. If they ignored the protesters, they looked weak; if they shot them, they looked like bullies.

Gandhi in South Africa

Gandhi went to work in Durban, South Africa, in 1893 and stayed in that country for twenty years. During that time he used non-cooperation and civil disobedience to protest at laws which discriminated against Indians.

For example, in 1907, a law required "Asiatics" to be fingerprinted and to carry a registration document at all times. Gandhi protested by disobeying: he refused to be fingerprinted, and for this was imprisoned.

In 1913, he was jailed again. This time, the South African government had said that Indians must not leave the province where they lived. And Gandhi had led 2,500 marchers from Natal into the Transvaal to demonstrate against the new law.

TEN THINGS YOU DIDN'T KNOW ABOUT MOHANDAS GANDHI

1. Gandhi was born in 1869. His father was Chief Minister to the Maharajah of Porbandar.

2. The name Gandhi means "grocer" (a reference to Gandhi's caste – the social group to which his family belonged).

3. In later life, Gandhi was called Mahatma, but this was a title, not his name. It means "Great Soul".

4. His mother belonged to a religion which forbade violence and eating meat. When he was a boy, Gandhi often smoked, ate meat, told lies and wore European clothes, but he always felt very guilty about it!

5. He studied law at London University and tried to set up a law practice in Bombay before he went to Durban, South Africa, in 1893, to work as a legal adviser for an Indian firm.

6. During the Boer War he organized an ambulance corps for the British Army and commanded a Red Cross unit.

7. When he led the Indian Independence movement, whatever the weather, he would always wear a simple loin cloth and shawl made from cloth that he had woven himself.

8. His policy of passive resistance was inspired partly by reading the works of Russian writer Leo Tolstoy.

9. He used fasting as another method of protest.

10. Gandhi's teachings later inspired the US civil rights leader Martin Luther King.

Gandhi returned to India in 1915 and became leader of the Indian National Congress party, which was pressing for home rule. His first Satyagraha campaign began after British troops had shot dead hundreds of protesters in Amritsar in 1919.

The Cloth Protest

One result of British rule in India was that local industries had been destroyed. For example, cloth was imported from Britain and so Indian spinners and weavers lost their livelihood. To symbolize his belief that Indian cottage industries should be revived, Gandhi would carry with him and use a spinning wheel.

In 1921, he called for a boycott of all cloth produced abroad. Foreign cloth was burned – which was bad news for mill workers in Lancashire, as most of their cloth was exported to India. For this and other protests, Gandhi was jailed from 1922-24. On his release, he continued his campaigns for the rights of women and of people called "Untouchables".

The Salt Tax

In 1930, Britain passed a law saying that tax would be charged on all the salt produced and sold in India. This presented Gandhi with a problem: in order to break the law, he would need to produce salt; but there were no salt mines where he lived at Ahmedabad.

The solution? He and his followers walked 300 kilometres to the sea, and made salt by distilling seawater. Thus they had broken the British law. Gandhi was jailed and his followers were brutally attacked by police, but the protests went on. And the salt tax was quickly lifted.

Western civilization

When asked what he thought of Western civilization, Gandhi is reported to have said:

"I think it would be a good idea."

Gandhi in London

Gandhi argued his case for Indian independence before the British parliament in 1931. Later he took tea with King George V (who as King of England was also the Emperor of India). Gandhi still wore his simple loin cloth and shawl for the occasion. The London weather had made the shawl dirty so he wore it inside out. When he returned to India, he was arrested again.

Quit India

In 1942, at the height of World War 2, the British government realized that it could no longer hold on to India. It offered to hand over rule after the war was over. Gandhi refused to wait and the Congress party asked Britain to quit India at once. Gandhi was arrested again. He took his spinning wheel to jail with him.

INDIA AND PAKISTAN

After World War 2 it still took two more years to work out how India should get its independence. If the government was going to be taken over by the Indian National Congress, led by Nehru, this would not be accepted by the Muslim League, led by Muhammad Ali Jinnah.

To solve the problem, it was necessary to split the country into Hindu India and Muslim Pakistan. Sadly, Gandhi had achieved his aim of gaining India's independence from Britain, but his other great cause of uniting the different Indian faiths had failed.

Independence had been achieved with little loss of life. But in the days that followed, 400,000 people were killed in fighting between Hindus and Muslims and over 8 million refugees left their homes to escape persecution. Gandhi himself survived for less then a year before being gunned down by a religious fanatic.

BANGLADESH

Pakistan consisted of East Pakistan and West Pakistan, one thousand miles apart. In 1971, East Pakistan broke away from West Pakistan to form the independent state of Bangladesh. India helped East Pakistan and wiped out half the Pakistani army and air force. The civil war was a human catastrophe.

In New York, a concert starring former Beatles George Harrison and Ringo Starr along with guitarist Eric Clapton and sitar player Ravi Shankar raised $250,000 in aid donations for the victims of the war.

Bangladesh achieved independence in 1972.

Kashmir

In 1947–49 and in 1965, India and Pakistan fought wars over the Northern territory of Kashmir. They solved nothing; Kashmir is still disputed territory.

AFRICA – THE WINDS OF CHANGE

In Africa, after World War 2, protests and guerilla campaigns began to convince the European powers that they could not hold on to their colonies there for much longer. In a speech to the South African parliament in 1960, British Prime Minister Harold Macmillan remarked:

"The wind of change is blowing through this continent."

His audience held on to their hats; they didn't want any such wind to affect them.

Independence for African states

1951	Libya
1956	Morocco, Sudan, Tunisia
1957	Ghana
1958	Guinea
1960	Cameroon, Central African Republic, Chad, Congo, Dahomey (Benin), Gabon, Ivory Coast, Madagascar, Mali, Mauritania, Niger, Nigeria, Senegal, Somalia, Togo, Upper Volta, Zaire
1961	Sierra Leone, Tanganyika (Tanzania)
1962	Algeria, Burundi, Rwanda, Uganda
1963	Kenya, Zanzibar
1964	Malawi, Zambia
1966	Botswana
1975	Angola, Mozambique
1980	Zimbabwe
1990	Namibia

After they became independent, most countries that had been part of the British Empire joined the Commonwealth.

THREE EXAMPLES OF AFRICAN INDEPENDENCE

Nigeria (independent 1960)
When pinching land for colonies, the Europeans had ignored tribal divisions. So, often, when a colony became independent, people from tribes that hated each other's guts found themselves in the same country. Elections left one tribe with power over another and this led to civil war.

In 1967, the Ibo tribe of Eastern Nigeria declared the breakaway republic of Biafra. A savage civil war lasted until 1970. Two million people died in the fighting or of starvation.

Asians expelled

Before independence, Indians had gone to work in British colonies in Africa. But, in 1969, the Kenyan government refused work permits to Asians and in 1972, Idi Amin expelled 20,000 Asians from Uganda. Many Kenyan and Ugandan Asians emigrated to Britain.

Kenya (independent 1963)
In 1951, members of the Kikuyu tribe formed the Mau Mau society. They launched a terrorist campaign against European settlers, which British troops were sent to quell.

The black nationalist leader, Jomo Kenyatta, was accused of leading the Mau Mau and jailed, though his real crime in the eyes of the authorities was that he had married an Englishwoman. Nine years later he was released and became the first President of independent Kenya.

Uganda (independent 1962)
Milton Obote, the first President, jailed ministers from minority tribes and assumed all powers. But he was deposed in 1970 by Idi Amin, a brutal psychopath, who immediately banned political activity and began a reign of terror. An estimated quarter of a million people died before Amin was thrown out after a war with Tanzania in 1979.

SOUTHERN AFRICA

In Southern Rhodesia and South Africa, the white settlers were strongly against handing over government to black leaders.

The white Rhodesian leader, Ian Smith, therefore made a Unilateral Declaration of Independence (UDI) from Britain in 1965. Britain responded by banning all trade with Rhodesia, but South Africa and other nations still supplied the rebel government, as did several major oil companies. Meanwhile, black freedom fighters led by Nelson Nkomo and Robert Mugabe harried the government. After a bitter armed struggle, the independent state of Zimbabwe was finally created in 1980, with Mugabe as Prime Minister.

South Africa and Apartheid

We saw how, at the end of the Boer War (page 10), the Afrikaners were allowed to keep their law denying the vote to black South Africans. In 1910, the Transvaal, Natal, Orange Free State and Cape Province joined together as the Union of South Africa – one of the British Dominions. White people were a minority of the population, but they made sure that they stayed absolutely in charge – for example, by passing laws like those that Gandhi encountered.

In 1948, laws were passed, systematizing the different treatment of different races. The system was called Apartheid. Some laws were simply childish: blacks had to use different toilets, buses and entrances to stores from white people.

Others were appalling:
Pass Laws: Black people could not live in, or even enter, white areas without a pass. Men were required to work in the mines, but their wives and children weren't allowed to go with them, so families were split up.
Land Acts: Black people were turned off their farms and tribal lands, and relocated to barren areas where nothing would grow.

Durban

Dear Uncle Oliver,
Am enjoying the seaside, but having separate beaches for black people and white people isn't fair. The beaches for whites are sandy and nearly empty, while the beaches for black people are stony and crowded. I saw nets round the white beaches and asked if the white people liked to fish, but the answer was that the nets are to protect white swimmers from sharks. There aren't any shark-nets for our beaches. I shall try to be careful while swimming.

Your loving nephew, Joe N'Soapi

South Africa v. the rest

South Africa declared itself a Republic in 1961, and Apartheid continued. The government was terrified by the move to independence throughout the rest of Africa. It was all very well for European powers to give their colonies independence; the whites there could just go home. But for Joe Van Der Soap, South Africa WAS home.

However, by the end of the 1980s, all but the most hard-line Afrikaners could see that there was no future for the white minority government.

This was a result of:
- international pressure
- sports boycotts
- trade restrictions
- civil unrest and strikes.

A happy ending?

It seems almost a miracle that when a black government finally came to power in 1993, under the leadership of Nelson Mandela, the feared backlash against white South Africans didn't happen. So far, the forgiveness and generosity of most black South Africans have set a standard that the rest of the world struggles to follow.

THE COLD WAR

In spite of their agreement at the end of World War 2, the USSR and the West very soon fell out. The split was between COMMUNISM and CAPITALISM.

The USSR had suffered terribly during the war. It wanted to set up Communist governments similar to its own in other Eastern European countries, as a defence against another invasion from the West. It believed that Capitalist countries like the USA would stop at nothing to destroy Communism.

The USA concluded that the USSR wanted to make the whole of Western Europe part of its Communist empire and then to make the rest of the world Communist too.

The complete division between East and West became known as **"The Iron Curtain"**.

The Berlin Wall

At the end of World War 2, Germany was split into four zones, controlled by the USA, Britain, France and the USSR. The German capital Berlin, in the USSR's zone, was similarly divided into four.

The divisions were not intended to last. However, conflict among the controllers led the British, French and US zones to form (Capitalist) West Germany in 1949, while the Russian zone became (Communist) East Germany.

West Berlin (a kind of island in the East) was part of West Germany. To stop contact between East and West, and to stop anyone crossing from one to the other (which was illegal), a huge, 29-mile-long concrete wall was built through the city in 1961. It was protected by minefields, machine gun towers and barbed wire.

NATO

In 1949 the North Atlantic Treaty Organization (NATO) was set up, to defend the West against the USSR. The countries that signed the treaty were: Belgium, Britain, Canada, Denmark, France, Iceland, Italy, Luxembourg, the Netherlands, Norway, Portugal and the USA – which had kept well out of European politics earlier in the century. In 1952, Greece and Turkey joined NATO; in 1955, West Germany; and in 1982, Spain.

Each country in NATO is agreed that an attack on any one of them will be understood as an attack on them all – and therefore they will all help to fight that attack as necessary.

The Warsaw Pact

In 1955, the USSR set up the Warsaw Pact as the Communist answer to NATO. Albania, Bulgaria, Czechoslovakia, East Germany, Hungary, Poland, Romania and the USSR were the countries who signed.

MADNESS

The USA had developed the atom bomb and used it to destroy Hiroshima and Nagasaki. In 1949, the USSR also exploded an atomic device. This meant that both "superpowers" had the capability of destroying each other with nuclear weapons - the situation was later called "MAD" (Mutual Assured Destruction).

Now it would have been too dangerous for the superpowers to go to war against each other directly. Instead, they expressed their differences by getting involved in smaller conflicts. By supporting one side or the other, they could each try to do the other down, without risking nuclear war.

THE KOREAN WAR, 1950-53

Communist North Korea v Democratic South Korea

Backed by:
the USSR
China

Backed by:
the UN (including the USA, Australia, Britain, etc)

When North Korea attacked South Korea in 1950, US General Douglas MacArthur's forces went to liberate the South Korean capital, Seoul. And then they crossed into North Korea, with the idea of freeing it too. However, Communist China sent a large army to help the North. The US and other UN forces were pushed back. Both sides dug in and, though there was savage fighting between the lines, neither could gain any advantage. Over 3 million Koreans and 88,000 UN troops were killed in this pointless war.

The only real result was that the USA had a new enemy: China.

COMMUNIST CHINA

During World War 2, Communists and Nationalists in China had combined to defeat the Japanese. But afterwards they renewed their fight for power. Civil war lasted until October 1, 1949, when the Communist leader, Mao Tse-tung declared the formation of the People's Republic of China. The defeated Nationalists, under Chiang Kai-shek, fled to the island of Taiwan and made cheap hi-fis.

Under Mao's leadership, China became a Communist state. Landlords were killed as land reform and co-operative farming were introduced. Like Stalin in Russia, Mao tried to modernize China through a series of plans.

Thought Reform

In the early 1950s Jao Zo-ping and his fellow Chinese citizens were made to condemn their old ways of thinking before committing themselves to the creation of a socialist society. Mao called this "re-education". The West called it "brainwashing".

The Great Leap Forward, 1958-61

This was a programme of industrialization. City-dwellers were forced into the countryside to become members of People's Communes and Production Brigades, helping to develop agriculture and build dams, reservoirs and backyard steel furnaces. The scheme failed and led to famine. 16 million died.

Feared

China and the USSR were the world's biggest Communist states and pally until 1960, when Mao fell out with the Russians over Communist ideology. The West was nervous and distrustful of the Chinese leadership; and there were wet beds in the American White House when China exploded an atom bomb in 1964. As Mao had hoped, China had become a world force that could not be brushed aside.

The Cultural Revolution, 1966-69

In the mid-1960s Mao wanted to return to the good old days of the revolution and to guide Jao Zo-ping back to the true socialist path. So he set out his ideas in his Little Red Book. This had nothing to do with grandmas eating wolves. It was a book of political action. People on buses were made to read it aloud, for example.

Red Guards were recruited and sent out to attack the four "olds" (old habits, old culture, old ideas and old customs) as a load of old rubbish. Thousands of people were killed or imprisoned, schools and colleges were closed down, and foreign powers were condemned.

The end of the century

Mao Tse-tung died in 1976. Events since then have shown a struggle between people who would Westernize and liberalize the country and people who want to prevent that change.

REDS UNDER THE BED

In the 1950s and '60s, Western governments were terrified of a Communist take-over. In the early 1950s Joe McCarthy, an American Senator, led a witch-hunt against "subversives" and "Communists" in the USA. Many ordinary people were arrested on suspicion of being Communists and questioned.

J. McCarthy: *Are you now, or have you ever been, a Communist?*
J. Soap: *No.*
J. McCarthy: *But your neighbour says he once saw you blow your nose on a red handkerchief.*
J. Soap: *Oh! What a fibber!*
J. McCarthy: *We'll lock you up and throw away the key. You'll never work again. Of course, we might let you go if you tell us about other Communists you know . . .*

Such hearings left a shameful scar on the USA.

MISSILE CRISIS

Cuba is an island off the coast of the USA and in 1959 it became a Communist state. In 1962, its President Fidel Castro, allowed the USSR to set up a missile base on the island, in return for Soviet aid. The USA wasn't prepared to have Soviet missiles in its own backyard and US President Kennedy demanded that the base be dismantled. For several weeks, until the Soviet leader Khrushchev backed down and recalled the missiles, the world teetered on the brink of nuclear war.

And next the USA got involved in Vietnam.

THE VIETNAM WAR

After it became independent from France in 1954, Vietnam was divided into the Communist "Democratic Republic" in the North and the "State" of Vietnam in the South. There was civil war, during which Communists fought a guerilla campaign against the corrupt government in the South. The guerillas were known as the Viet Cong.

The USA believed that if South Vietnam fell under Communist control, other Asian countries would follow. This was known as the "domino theory". President Kennedy therefore sent more than 16,000 US troops to help South Vietnam. They were called "advisers", to avoid clashes with China and the USSR.

In 1965 the USA began a huge bombing campaign against North Vietnam and sent an army of 50,000 to "protect US airfields". The bombing didn't work. The Viet Cong fought from underground shelters and made lightning raids on US bases from neighbouring Cambodia. So the USA sent in more troops from South Korea, Thailand, Australia and New Zealand, and yet they still couldn't beat the Viet Cong. In desperation, the USA then began to use cruel and dreadful new chemical weapons including:

- **Napalm**: an inflammable, jelly-like substance designed to stick to the body and burn

- **Agent Orange** and other defoliants. These plant-killing chemicals destroyed the jungles used as cover by the Viet Cong, and also the rice crop.

THE NAME'SH ORANGE. AGENT ORANGE.

LICENSHED TO DEFOLIATE.

Drafted in

In the second half of the 1960s, young Americans were "drafted" to join the half a million US soldiers already involved in Vietnam. Opposition to the war grew, especially after a Viet Cong offensive sent US casualty figures rocketing to over a thousand deaths a month.

In 1970, US President Nixon decided to attack Viet Cong bases in neighbouring countries. US forces were sent across the border to Cambodia. A hundred thousand anti-war protesters marched on Washington and students held strikes and sit-ins.

Kent State University, 1970

Dear President Nixon

I am writing to ask you please to stop the war in Vietnam. You drafted my brother into the army and he got killed. I joined a student protest at my University and the National Guard shot dead six students because they wanted the war stopped. Why should Americans die for something that is happening halfway round the world? Bring our boys home. Please.

Yours sincerely

Jo-Ann Soapechne (18)

Withdrawn at last

US soldiers became convinced that they were fighting a war that the USA should never have got involved in and couldn't win. They turned to drink and drugs. They got rid of unpopular officers by "fragging" them (blowing them to bits with a fragmentation grenade). Black soldiers were fed up with fighting what they saw as a "white man's war". **Vietnam Veterans**, finding themselves treated as criminals, set up their own anti-war protest. At last, US troops were pulled out of Vietnam in 1972, though the bombing continued.

A war lost on TV

Scenes from Vietnam were shown in colour on TV news, and so people at home and far from the fighting knew much more about this war than they would ever have done in the past. In earlier times, war reports in the media might have drummed up popular support. But the Vietnam TV reports had the opposite effect. It was said that the war was "lost in the living rooms of America – not on the battlefields of Vietnam".

The fall of Saigon

In 1974, President Nixon was forced to resign after the **Watergate** scandal (he was apparently involved in efforts to steal information from his Democratic Party rival in the 1972 presidential election). With its last friend in the US gone, the South Vietnamese government surrendered following the fall of Saigon in April 1975.

Vietnam Troops

	Number of troops	Number killed
South Vietnamese Army	7 million	224,000
US Army	2.6 million	58,000
Viet Cong	Unknown	900,000

THE END OF THE COLD WAR

Weapons technology became more and more frightening. In the 1950s the hydrogen bomb was developed, many times more destructive than the atom bomb. While the bomb that destroyed Hiroshima had a force of about 12 megatons (12,000 tons of TNT), a large hydrogen bomb might have 1 million megatons.

Nuclear weapons can be delivered by all kinds of means. There are:
- land-based Intercontinental Ballistic Missiles (ICBMs)
- Submarine-Launched Ballistic Missiles (SLBMs)
- Cruise missiles launched from aircraft
- MIRVED missiles carrying multiple warheads, which can destroy a number of targets at once.

There are also neutron bombs, which kill people but leave buildings standing.

In the 1980s, the USA planned the Strategic Defence Initiative (Star Wars), a satellite defence system against ICBMs.

A Pinch of SALT

The danger and cost of American and Russian weapons programmes spiralled out of control. The Strategic Arms Limitation (SALT) agreements of 1972 and 1974, between the USA and the USSR, began a process of arms reduction. And yet, by 1990, the two nations together had 50,000 nuclear warheads.

However, trying to keep up with the USA bankrupted the USSR and in 1991 the country collapsed. This is what finally brought the Cold War to an end.

hopeful

As the 20th century closes, both superpowers are destroying their stocks of nuclear weapons. We can only hope that this will end the period of madness during which the two most powerful nations on Earth had the power to wipe the whole human race from the planet.

BOOM!

Rationing continued for a while after the end of World War 2, but soon Joe and Josephine Soap became much better off.

"WE'VE NEVER HAD IT SO GOOD!"

Exciting challenges were met in the 1950s and 1960s:
- Edmund Hillary (a bee-keeper from New Zealand) and Tenzing Norgay conquered the world's highest mountain, Everest, in 1953. (As Tenzing said at the time, "Done the bugger!")
- Jacques Cousteau and Auguste and Jacques Piccard investigated the mysteries of the deep oceans . . .
- The first artificial satellite, Sputnik 1, was launched by the USSR in 1957.
- The first human in space, Russian Yuri Gagarin, orbited the earth in 1961.
- In 1969, Americans Neil Armstrong and Buzz Aldrin walked on the moon.

Back on Earth, spectacular changes took place in society.

GOOD HEALTH!

The National Health Service was set up in Britain in 1948. Its aim was to give everyone in Britain, rich and poor:
- free health care
- free dental care
- free glasses
- and even free wigs!

It would all be paid for out of the money people paid in taxes. At first, doctors didn't want to work for the National Health Service and threatened to go on strike, but later most became committed supporters of the system.

Medical news

1953 Polio vaccine produced.
1953 DNA discovered.
1956 Hormones discovered.
1957 The first artificial heart invented in the USA.
1958 The pacemaker invented.
1962 Lasers first used to correct bad eyesight.
1967 First human heart transplant.

21st-century health

At the end of the 20th century the Health Service is in trouble. Many new treatments that are developed for serious diseases and injuries are incredibly expensive. People are having to wait a long time for treatment and sometimes even emergency cases cannot find a bed. The state of the NHS is going to be a big issue for government in the 21st century.

SQUARE EYES

Television sets became available from the 1950s. Soon, the Soaps, who once went out to the movies three times a week, could have their very own picture show right in their living room. It was only in black and white, of course, and the picture was about 20 cm across and could give you heatstroke if you sat too close!

What they saw on the news, 1950s and 1960s

Exciting: Men in space and on the moon. The Beatles.

Hopeful: Coronation of Queen Elizabeth II, 1953. Martin Luther King's peaceful campaign for equal rights for black people in the USA.

Terrible: Wars in Israel, Biafra, Vietnam. Spillage of oil from *Torrey Canyon* tanker, 1967. Landslip of mining waste, Aberfan, 1966, killing 144. Assassinations of John F. Kennedy, 1963, and Martin Luther King, 1968.

Confusing: Western and Soviet spies being arrested.

Some British TV dates

- **1936** Start of BBC TV service.
- **1955** ITV started broadcasting.
- **1964** BBC2 went on air.
- **1967** Colour TV.
- **1974** Teletext first used.
- **1982** Start of Channel 4.
- **1983** Breakfast TV first broadcast.
- **1989** First Sky satellite broadcasts.

It went off for an hour in the evening, so that Ma and Pa Soap could put the little Soaps to bed. The only daytime broadcasts were schools programmes and the Test Card, a picture surrounded by patterns which helped engineers tune televisions in. Nonetheless, by 1959, there were 24.5 million TV sets in Britain.

TEENAGERS

Before the 1950s, teenage just didn't exist. You went from being a child to being an adult. When you finished school you got a job or an apprenticeship and gave your wages to your mum. But as prosperity increased, the school leaving age was raised . . . and suddenly teenagers appeared on the scene. Industries were created to sell things to them: mostly clothes and records, but also zit-cream - from which drugs companies made a fortune.

Teenagers were rebellious, like characters played by US film stars James Dean and Marlon Brando who created the image of the surly, antisocial scruff wearing ripped shirts, tight jeans and a sneer. The '50s and '60s saw the rise of teen culture; first Teddy Boys, then Mods and Rockers trashed seaside towns on Bank Holidays. More thoughtful teenagers joined protest groups against the war in Vietnam, racism and the arms race.

The Yanks Are Coming!

US servicemen stationed in Britain during World War 2 were a novelty. They gave women presents of nylon stockings and perfume, whereas the best that British men could offer was cotton socks and coal tar soap. (Jealous British males described the American GIs as "Overpaid, Over-sexed and Over Here"!)

After the war, the American influence flooded Europe. As the USA felt more confident about itself, film producers switched from making movies about English history to making pictures about American life. TV producers followed suit, and British companies queued to buy US shows, like *I Love Lucy*, *The Beverly Hillbillies* and *The Dick Van Dyke Show* (he's the one with the funny accent in Maowry Pawppins).

Teenagers especially picked up American culture because it offered more freedom than the stuffy ideas of their elders.

WOMEN AT WORK

During World War 2 (in the same way as during World War 1) women had done "men's jobs", while the men were away fighting. They had worked in factories, driven lorries and even flown planes. But this time, when Joe returned saying "Ta very much. I'll take over now. Nip back home and put the treacle pudding on to steam," he was surprised to find that Josephine wasn't having any. She wanted to keep her paid work and her new independence.

Women Prime Ministers

Sirimavo Bandaranaike, Sri Lanka, 1960-65; 1970-77

Benazir Bhutto, Pakistan, 1988-90

Indira Gandhi, India, 1966-77; 1980-84

Golda Meir, Israel, 1969-74

Margaret Thatcher, Britain, 1979-90

New labour-saving devices (like washing machines and vacuum cleaners) and convenience foods meant that housework didn't take as long as it used to. Women had more time to look around and think, "Hmmmmm. . .". They began to demand equal rights to jobs and pay.

Another thing enabling women to think along these lines was the development of the birth control pill.

The situation today

In Britain, the Equal Pay Act was passed in 1970, and in 1975 the Sex Discrimination Act made it illegal not to give women equal opportunities in employment, education and other areas. Since then women have reached many top positions in government and industry. However, as women form roughly 50 per cent of the population, they should hold about half of the top jobs, and they don't. The figure is nearer 5 per cent. There's clearly a long way still to go for Women's Liberation.

THINGS JAPANESE

World War 2 left Japan in a mess. Two of its cities had been flattened by nuclear bombs, and hundreds of thousands of people had died in the fighting. Worst of all, the Japanese had lost their faith. Japan was a strict society in which Jokomoto Soapiyama was used to being told what to do by powerful leaders. But those leaders - even the Emperor, who had been looked on as a god - had lost the war.

Instead of crying into their sake, the Japanese decided that, if they weren't the best in the world at fighting wars, they'd be the best in the world at something else. Japan has virtually no raw materials, and its industries had been ruined; so what could be more natural than to decide to become the world's best at making things?!

All change

The secret of Japan's success is precisely that when it began to rebuild, it was able to start completely afresh. Western countries tried to protect their old-fashioned industries and change gradually; but Japan had no industry left to protect, and so it could change faster.

Take motorbikes: In Britain, motorbikes were made by a number of old-fashioned companies. They had wonderful old-fashioned names like Enfield and Matchless; cost three years' salary; and fell to bits every 200 miles. But this didn't matter because, if Joe Soap wanted a motorbike, these were the best he could get.

Then the Japanese started exporting motorbikes to Britain. They were much cheaper than British bikes. Better still, they didn't fall to bits. Britain's motorbike industry went into a nosedive and never recovered.

The same thing happened in shipbuilding, and in every sort of electronics industry (hi-fi, TV, video, etc). At the end of the 20th century Japan has the second highest gross national product in the world.

How to achieve an Economic Miracle

- Copy Western designs, but then improve on them.
- Use cheap labour from poorer neighbouring countries.
- Make your factories more efficient.
- Reward good work and good ideas.
- Train people well and then pay them properly.
- Be very, very competitive.

Japan's miracle hasn't been achieved without cost. Society is very regulated. Getting into the best universities is harder than getting into the Cup Final without a ticket. Teenagers commit suicide over poor exam results. However, by spending lots on research and cutting costs, Japan is likely to be a major economic power well into the 21st century.

THE GOOD ASSASSINATION GUIDE 2

One thing that didn't seem to change during the century was the fashion for assassination. Here's who was Top Of the Hit Parade from 1945 onwards:

YEAR	NAME	POSITION	CAUSE OF DEATH
1948	Mahatma Gandhi	Indian leader	Shot by a Hindu fanatic in Delhi.
1963	John F. Kennedy	US President	Shot in Dallas supposedly by Lee Harvey Oswald.
1968	Martin Luther King	US black Civil Rights leader	Shot in Memphis by a white man, James Earl Ray.
1978	Aldo Moro	Former Italian Prime Minister	Kidnapped and shot by terrorists.
1979	Louis Mountbatten	Member of British Royal Family	Blown up by IRA bomb whilst sailing.
1981	Anwar Sadat	Egyptian President	Shot dead in Cairo by Islamic extremists.
1984	Indira Gandhi	Indian Prime Minister	Shot by her Sikh bodyguards.
1986	Olaf Palme	Swedish Prime Minister	Shot in Stockholm by lone gunman.
1995	Itzhak Rabin	Israeli Prime Minister	Shot by Jewish extremist.

... AND BUST

The boom years ended in 1973. War with Israel led the Arab countries in the Organization of Petroleum Exporting Countries (OPEC) to put up the price of oil by 70 per cent, to put pressure on the USA and other Western countries who were thought to be pro-Israel. In Britain, the massive hike in oil prices coincided with a miners' strike. Power was cut to homes for hours at a time, and industry closed for four days out of every seven. Because petrol was in short supply, motorists were urged to keep their speed down to 50 mph – it was almost back to rationing.

The confidence of the 1950s and 1960s was replaced by uncertainty and confusion. There had been a clear goal in 1945 - to rebuild a world ravaged by war. Now that had been done – sort of. Where was there to go now?

QUIZ
WHAT WAS INVENTED?
1940 - 1999

1. ENIAC was built for the US Army by John Mauchly and John Eckert in 1946. It filled a room, but nowadays everything it did can be done by a device that can fit in the palm of your hand.

2. The EBR-1 was American and the first of its kind. A new way of producing energy, but is it e-fission-t? And is it safe?

3. Why did the stripey horse cross the road in 1951? To get to the chicken on the other side?

4. They were invented in 1958 by Jack St Kilby, and these days, you get them with everything.

5. Designed by Christopher Cockerell in 1959, this vehicle's departures are described as "flights", but it never rises more than a few centimetres from the surface.

6. First produced in 1959, this has lots of uses: reading bar codes, operating on eyes, playing CDs, and cutting secret agents in half in James Bond movies.

7. In 1961 the Dutch company Phillips made this smaller device for capturing the voice.

8. This went sky-high in 1962 and bounced TV pictures between continents.

9. Developed by Texas Instruments to help mathematical numbskulls add, subtract, divide and multiply without having to take off their shoes and socks when dealing with numbers between 11 and 20. Thank you, thank you, Texas!

10. The first (in 1970) was number 747. Did it have two big ears and a trunk?

11. First marketed in 1970, it allows you to watch one awful TV programme whilst recording another. Hurray!

12. Try writing its number down sitting on a platform in your anorak, holding your flask of milky tea with three sugars and packet of fish paste sandwiches, as it whizzes past at 380 km per hour. The French have had it since 1978. Britain is still waiting!

13. Moving music? Next time you're driven mad on a bus by a bum-bum-bum noise, blame Akio Morita's 1979 invention.

14. Developed by the Phillips and Sony companies and launched in the early 1980s, they're damned hard to scratch, but make an incredible phizzing and cracking noise if you microwave one. (Please don't try this at home - try it at your friend's!*)
* Only kidding.

(Answers on page 124)

CONTINUING CONFLICTS

Wars going on at the end of the century are smaller, but no less cruel and bloody, than the two World Wars. The issues behind them are more confusing and perhaps more difficult to solve.

THE ARAB-ISRAELI WARS

During World War 1, in return for their help in fighting Germany, the British government promised British Jews a home of their own in Palestine. After the war, when Britain was given the job of looking after Palestine (which had been part of the Turkish empire), the promise was conveniently forgotten.

There were already 50,000 Jews living in Palestine, but there were also half a million Arabs. For both groups, the country was their Holy Land. Britain hadn't thought what would happen to the Arabs when more Jews moved in. Understandably, the Palestinian Arabs weren't best pleased to find Britain running their country after the war. The British said that by "home", they didn't mean a "state".

Thousands of Jewish immigrants arrived in the 1920s and 1930s, especially after Hitler came to power in Germany and they needed refuge. Alarmed at the numbers, the Palestinian Arabs began a campaign of strikes and attacks on Jewish and British targets. The Jews retaliated.

Partition plans

The idea of dividing Palestine was first proposed in 1937; two thirds of the territory was to go to the Arabs, and one third to the Jews. Neither side was happy with this.

Then, as the sufferings of Jews in Germany and Eastern Europe at the hands of the Nazis became clear, the UN decided that 100,000 Jews would be allowed to move to Palestine in 1946. The Jews said "not enough"; the Arabs said "too many". Ships carrying Jewish refugees from Europe were prevented from landing by British warships.

In 1947, Britain decided to pull out, because it was skint and couldn't afford to keep troops in the Middle East. Taking over Britain's responsibility, the UN decided that the partition of Palestine should go ahead. Violence increased.

The creation of Israel

Eight hours before the British were due to pull out, the Jews proclaimed the new state of Israel. The USA immediately announced its support for the new state. Israel's Arab neighbours mobilized their forces.

THE WAR OF 1948-49: Palestinian Arabs, with the help of neighbouring countries Egypt and Iraq, tried (and failed) to throw the newcomers out. The Egyptians and Iraqis attacked Jewish targets but encountered stiff resistance. Faced with the threat of UN sanctions, they withdrew, leaving Israel larger than before. Israel was recognized by Britain, and became a member of the United Nations, in 1949.

THE WAR OF 1956: This was caused when Egypt wanted to control the Suez canal. Britain and France high-handedly invaded Egypt, and Israel took the opportunity to attack Egypt across the Sinai peninsula while its armed forces were busy in Suez. The USA was furious at the invasion and threatened to bankrupt Britain's shaky economy unless the British and French withdrew. Humiliated, Britain was forced to pull out.

THE SIX DAY WAR, 1967:
Convinced that Egypt, Syria and Jordan were about to declare war again, Israel got its blow in first and captured: the Gaza strip, Bethlehem, Hebron, Jerusalem, Jericho, the West Bank and the Golan Heights. It now controlled a territory many times larger than its own, and 1,500,000 Arabs found themselves living under Israeli rule and not liking it one bit.

THE YOM KIPPUR WAR, 1973: Neither side gained any real advantage in this war. Egypt and Syria attacked during the most holy day in the Jewish calendar. Israeli forces were taken by surprise, but quickly regrouped and drove the invaders back.

Continuing tensions

The Palestinian Arabs realized that they were unlikely to beat Israel in a straight battle. Instead they turned to the Palestine Liberation Organization (PLO), to keep up pressure on Israel with a guerilla war.

The PLO was based in Lebanon, where there was already civil war between Christian and Muslim groups. In 1982, Israel made matters worse by invading Lebanon to knock out PLO bases. Once rich and peaceful, the country became a battlefield. Atrocity followed atrocity, eventually leading to the hostage crises that saw John McCarthy, Terry Waite and others captured and held for five years by Israel's enemies.

Tensions continue in the Middle East. During the Gulf War, Sadam Hussein tried to break up the coalition of his enemies by launching rocket attacks on Israel. He hoped that the Israelis would come into the war, and that the Arab members of the coalition would withdraw rather than fight on Israel's side. It nearly worked.

Hopefully, Israel's withdrawal from some of the captured territories and its agreement with PLO leader Yasser Arafat marks the beginning of a longer-lasting peace. However, as the 20th century ends, the prospects of a reconciliation between Jews and Arabs seem as far away as ever.

WAR IN THE GULF

Other Arab nations were infected by the mood of anger surrounding the creation of Israel. In 1978, Iran (formerly Persia) kicked out its traditional sovereign, the Shah, in favour of the extremist Muslim leader Ayatollah Khomeini.

When Iraq then came under the control of military dictator Sadam Hussein in 1979, conflict between Iran and Iraq was inevitable. They were traditionally enemies. So, in 1980, they went to war for no better reason than to see who would come out on top. In fact, neither did. Eight years of bloody fighting left a million dead, including the passengers and crew of an Iranian airliner shot down by an American warship by mistake. The USA had wanted Iraq to win. Although Iraq was friendly with the USSR, the Americans reckoned that it was better than Iran, which wasn't friendly with anyone and had kept the US embassy staff in Tehran imprisoned for over a year. But US feeling changed right about, when Saddam Hussein invaded Kuwait in 1991.

The UN agreed with US President Bush that this was a no-no, and that Iraq should be kicked out. This would be done by a military Coalition of 31 countries.

Saddam's enemies

The UN military Coalition consisted of:

Argentina	Denmark	Netherlands	Saudi Arabia
Australia	Egypt	New Zealand	Senegal
Bahrain	France	Niger	South Korea
Bangladesh	Greece	Norway	Spain
Belgium	Hungary	Oman	Syria
Britain	Italy	Pakistan	United Arab Emirates
Canada	Kuwait	Poland	
Czechoslovakia	Morocco	Qatar	USA

Human shields

Saddam declared that Kuwait was "eternally" a part of Iraq. He tried to stop the Coalition forces fighting back by using Western hostages captured during the invasion as "human shields": placing them around possible targets for military action. As more Arab nations joined the Coalition in disgust at Saddam's tactics, he released the hostages.

Desert Storm

The Coalition attacked, in no half-hearted way. They bombed Saddam's capital, Baghdad, and destroyed most of the Iraqi air force. Over a month, they flew nearly 100,000 bombing raids, and this was followed by a land offensive lasting only 100 hours.

The Coalition used saturation bombing with conventional weapons and napalm, and shells tipped with uranium. Bulldozers were brought in to bury Iraqi troops alive in their trenches. Horrified at the ease with which their troops were wiping out the Iraqi army, Coalition leaders declared a ceasefire.

Iraq, for its part, massacred Kuwaiti civilians, set fire to Kuwaiti oilfields and released oil into the sea, causing appalling environmental damage.

The war cost relatively few lives (around 300) among the US-led forces. Estimates vary as to how many Iraqis died: not fewer than 100,000; perhaps as many as 250,000. Fleeing from their reign of terror in Kuwait, tens of thousands of Iraqi soldiers were massacred on the Basra road.

President Bush decided not to pursue the Iraqi forces into Iraq. Saddam Hussein remained in power, but with his armed forces badly weakened.

Weird War 1
What was the Cod War, 1973-76?
Not, unfortunately, a fight to the death between shoals of cod and herring armed with machine guns, but a dispute over fishing rights between Britain and Iceland.

NORTHERN IRELAND

Here's a quick run-down of how the Irish "Troubles" had developed by the start of the 20th century. Ready?

Protestants in

In Tudor times, Ireland was taken over by the English crown. During the reign of the first Stuart King, James I, the Catholic Irish aristocracy legged it to Spain. Their land, especially in the northern part of Ireland, was taken over by English and Scottish Protestant landowners. So now, most of the landowners in Ireland were English Protestants, but most of their tenants were Irish Catholics.

Following so far?

The Battle of the Boyne

Under James II (who was Catholic), the Catholics did rather better. But James was driven from England and then defeated in Ireland by Protestant Prince William of Orange ("King Billy") in 1690 at the Battle of the Boyne. Though this happened 300 years ago, the Protestant Orange Order still celebrates the battle every year by marching through Catholic areas (which some might term tactless).

Governed from London

Following a Catholic rebellion in 1798, the government of Ireland was shifted from Dublin to London in 1801. To add insult to injury, only Protestants could be elected to the London Parliament.

Potatoes

The seal was set on Catholic bitterness by a natural catastrophe. Potatoes formed 90 per cent of the Irish diet. When a disease destroyed the potato crop in three successive years in the 1840s, hundreds of thousands of Irish people starved to death. Many more emigrated. The population went down by a quarter.

Many Irish Catholics who settled in the USA felt bitter against Britain, for doing so little to help the sufferings of the Irish. This explains why many Irish Americans in the 20th century are keen supporters of the IRA.

The early 20th century

As the 20th century began, Catholic Nationalists in Ireland were calling for "Home Rule". Protestant Unionists (who wanted Ireland to stay "united" with Britain) replied that "Home Rule" meant "Rome Rule". Many Irish still fought for Britain during World War 1.

After the war, however, the newly-formed Irish Republican Army made the anti-British feeling more obvious. They fought the police and the British Army. Elections were held in which the party of the Nationalists, Sinn Fein, won a huge majority. And, instead of taking their seats in London, they set up a parliament in Dublin.

Partition

In 1921, the British government gave in. Most of Northern Ireland (Ulster) was to remain part of Britain, but the rest of Ireland became the Irish Free State. (It was a Dominion, like Canada and Australia.)

The Republic of Ireland

The partition was never going to be a final solution. Resentment smouldered on both sides.

In World War 2, the Irish Free State remained neutral. The British government and the Ulster Protestants saw this as a betrayal and even accused the Irish Free State of providing a base for Nazi spies. In 1949, the Free State declared itself a Republic.

The Easter Rising

Just before the start of World War 1, the British government promised the Irish Home Rule. This satisfied some people and many Irish regiments served with the British Army in the war. But the Nationalists did not wait: at Easter, 1916, they raised a rebellion in Dublin and declared an Irish republic. The rebellion was a failure and its leaders were all executed.

Catholics in the North

After 1949, there were still plenty of Catholics in Northern Ireland, but Unionists saw to it that election boundaries were arranged so that Protestants were in the majority in each district. Catholics were discriminated against. They found it hard to get good jobs, get council houses, or join the police.

British troops and paramilitaries

In the late 1960s, Catholics in Northern Ireland protested increasingly about the way they were treated. In 1969, Catholic marchers were attacked by Protestants. Because the mainly Protestant police force did nothing to help the Catholics, British troops were sent to defend them.

At first, the troops were welcomed; but suspicions grew that they had really come to make sure that Northern Ireland stayed British. The Provisional IRA broke away from the main Republican movement and began a campaign to kill British soldiers. The Protestants responded by forming the Ulster Defence Association (UDA). Many other paramilitary organizations have been formed.

Terrorism

In 1972, the British government suspended the Northern Irish parliament and began to rule the province directly from London. Catholics and Protestants set in for a campaign of terrorism. In 1992, the death toll in the "Troubles" had reached 3,000. A short-lived ceasefire ended in 1996, and the conflict goes on.

Weird War 2

Who fought in the Soccer War, 1969?
Fighting on and off the pitch began when El Salvador played a football match against Honduras in 1969. Two weeks later, El Salvador's troops invaded Honduras and its planes bombed the airport. Oooo, Ref, that was dirty !!!

BOSNIA

The break-up of the USSR in 1991 ended the Cold War, but it wasn't all good news.

People find it hard to understand what's going on in Bosnia. Let's put it this way:

1. Suppose you took all the football supporters from, say, Millwall, Chelsea, Liverpool, Manchester United and Glasgow Rangers.
2. You put them in one football ground and tell them that they all now have to support the same team.
3. You put lots of armed guards around the ground to make sure they behave.
4. You take the guards away.

See?

This is roughly what happened in Yugoslavia. At the end of World War 2, Yugoslavia was created as a federal state consisting of six republics: Serbia, Croatia, Slovenia, Bosnia-Herzegovina, Macedonia and Montenegro. The people of these republics, Serbs, Croats, Muslims and other ethnic groups, had a history of hating each other, but managed to get along under the leadership of the Communist leader Tito. They also had a common enemy: the USSR.

Then Tito died in 1980 and the tensions between the republics began to show. And when the USSR collapsed in 1991, the racial tensions exploded and civil war broke out in Yugoslavia.

In most of the breakaway states, one group or another was dominant. Croatia and Slovenia became new countries. However, it was Bosnia's misfortune to be a hotch-potch of all the peoples who had made up Yugoslavia - and they all wanted to control the government.

A bloody and bitter conflict took place between Serbs, Croats and Muslims. There followed the horrors of the siege of Sarajevo, Serbian death camps and "ethnic cleansing" (which is a polite way of referring to racial killings). Finally, after months of dithering, the UN unleashed a series of punishing air strikes on the Serbs.

The ceasefire which was put in place in 1995 and enforced by NATO may have ended the war; but at the moment this is a hope, not a result.

The break-up of the USSR

An important figure in the breaking up of the USSR was Mikhail Gorbachev. He was General Secretary of the Communist Party and became President of the USSR in 1988.

He brought about huge changes to Soviet society, by restructuring the economy and making political and cultural affairs more open. Contact with the West was opened up and this put an end to the suspicions between East and West that had started the Cold War.

Gorbachev allowed the republics of the USSR to become independent and resigned as President in 1991.

THE END OF THE CENTURY

The World Wars dominated the first half of the century. War was probably the outside event that most threatened to upset the lives of Joe and Josephine Soap. By the end of the century this was no longer the case. There was lots to feel hopeful and excited about, along with new terrible concerns.

COLLAPSING COMMUNISM

When Mikhail Gorbachev was introducing his reforms to the USSR in the late 1980s and making life there more relaxed, other countries in Eastern Europe were affected too. Their governments had been backed by the old USSR and were used to keeping strict control over their people. Without the USSR in the background, they began to lose that control. In Poland, Solidarity, a trade union, was elected to power in 1989. In Hungary, reforms similar to Gorbachev's were allowed, but in Romania and Czechoslovakia, the Communist leaders would not budge.

... and a collapsing wall

The Communist government in East Germany fell in 1989, and in 1990 East and West Germany were reunited. The rest of the world looked on with amazement as the Berlin Wall was taken down, and Berlin - once again - became the capital of Germany.

EUROPEAN UNION

In 1991, Belgium, Denmark, France, Germany, Greece, Ireland, Luxembourg, the Netherlands, Portugal, Spain, Italy and the UK formed the European Union (EU), created under the Maastricht Treaty. Austria, Finland and Sweden joined in 1994. The aim is to build a peaceful Europe.

Joe Soap and his friends probably find that the main result of the European Union is that they can drive the Volvo onto a Chunnel train, load up with cheap booze at a Calais hypermarket until the suspension creaks, bring it back to the UK and not have to pay.

But if they think about it and compare the relationships in Europe now with what they were like 50 or 60 years ago, they can't deny that the politicians have achieved something!

Steps to European Union

After World War 2, European politicians realized that, since no single European state could match the USA or USSR for political or industrial muscle, it was time to forget old rivalries and learn to work together. The French set the ball rolling by setting up the European Coal and Steel Community (ECSC) whose members agreed a customs union and a free-trade area.

Treaty of Paris (1951) created the ECSC.

Treaties of Rome (1957) created the European Economic Community (EEC or Common Market).

Merger Treaty (1965) established a government for the whole of Europe:

- the Council of Ministers
- the European Commission
- the European Parliament
- the Court of Justice
- the European Council.

European Single Act (1986) and **Maastricht Treaty** (December 1991) allowed for the creation of a single currency (the ECU: European Currency Unit), a European Central Bank, and community-wide citizenship.

Willkommen England, Bienvenue Angleterre, etc, etc

Britain joined the Community along with Ireland and Denmark in 1973, having been kept out during the 1960s by President de Gaulle of France, who thought that Britain's ties with the Commonwealth and the USA would cause difficulties, and anyway didn't like Britain much.

At the end of the 20th century, membership of the EU has become a major issue in British politics. Some politicians want to hold a referendum, to find out from Joe and Josephine Soap what they think of the idea of earning and spending ECUs instead of pounds.

HEALTH

hopeful

On the whole, Joe Soap and his friends in the developed countries now live longer and are healthier than at any time before. In 1900, if people reached the age of 44 they were doing well. Today, they can expect to live about 80 years because:

- More is known about how Joe's and Josephine's bodies work.
- Knowledge about disease and its prevention has grown phenomenally.
- New "wonder" drugs have been discovered and developed.
- Technological progress has produced life-saving machines.
- People are better educated about health issues.
- Living conditions are cleaner.

In 1900, the leading causes of death in the Western World were consumption (tuberculosis), pneumonia, cholera, measles, cancer, typhoid, diphtheria, whooping cough and scarlet fever. Most of these are now easily treated and not life threatening.

Thanks to the development of psychology, we know much more about the workings of the brain and can treat people with mental disorders through psychoanalysis. Drugs can also help people with mental illnesses.

terrible

Whilst so many diseases have been defeated, new ones are appearing. And some old ones seem to be re-appearing, having worked out how to beat the antibiotics.

AIDS (Acquired Immune Deficiency Syndrome) is a new disease of the 20th century. It is a viral infection that attacks the immune system. It can be passed on through sexual contact. Although it seems that the disease has been present since the 1950s, it was not recognized until the 1980s. It is estimated that over 10 million people worldwide have died from AIDS so far. A cure has not yet been found.

THE ENVIRONMENT

Up until the 1980s, if Joe and Josephine Soap went protesting, it was probably against war, or against nuclear weapons. For instance, Josephine and lots of other women went to Greenham Common, to demonstrate against the US nuclear missile base there. At the end of the century, the issues that people demonstrated about became environmental.

Increasingly, events showed that all the century's technological progress was damaging or using up the earth's resources.

Air pollution

Car exhausts and smoke from home and industrial chimneys have polluted the air (especially with Carbon Dioxide), leading to problems with:

The O Zone: The ozone layer which shelters us from the Sun's radiation has been severely damaged. (Slap that Factor 20 sun block on!)

Global Warming: The effect of the Carbon Dioxide on the atmosphere has been to trap heat reflected from the earth, causing temperatures to rise all over the world. This will lead the seas to rise and flood low-lying areas. (Bye bye, London!)

Trees and plants use Carbon Dioxide to grow. They breathe it in and breathe out oxygen. So lots of trees would help the Global Warming problem. BUT . . . the world's biggest areas of trees, the rainforests, have been destroyed (and burned), to make room for cattle ranches and roads - and into the bargain, burning trees produces . . . yep! You guessed it! Lots of lovely Carbon Dioxide.

Desert, anyone?

The world's deserts are expanding, as a result partly of Global Warming and the climate change it causes and partly of overintensive grazing of livestock and planting of crops. Famines in the 1980s in Ethiopia and the Sudan drew attention to the problem.

Energy

To run their cars and homes and industries, 20th-century people needed increasing amounts of energy, produced mostly by burning coal, gas and oil. These fuels don't just cause pollution - but also will run out. Then how will the Soaps keep warm and get about? Generations to come will probably use "alternative" energy sources: wind, solar, wave power, etc - and bikes.

Oil's well that ends well. . . ?

Oil is transported around the world in tankers. If it spills into the sea, it causes ugly and dangerous damage. This was seen when the following oil tankers had accidents:
1967 the *Torrey Canyon* (off Cornwall)
1989 the *Exxon Valdez* (Alaska)
1993 the *Braer* (The Shetlands)
1996 the *Sea Empress* (South Wales).

Why don't oil tanker drivers look where they're going?!

Nuclear fallout

Nuclear power is an alternative energy source. The arguments for it are that it is cheap and clean. But is it safe? In 1979 there was an accident at the Three Mile Island nuclear power station in the USA, which nearly led to "meltdown" of the reactor core. In April 1986 an accident at a nuclear power station in Chernobyl in the Ukraine really did spread radiation across Europe. Even if accidents don't happen, reactors produce radioactive waste that remains deadly for thousands of years. No-one seems sure where it is going to be stored.

Is the future back in the past?

Seeing that modern technology was not all good, increasing numbers of people have looked back at old ways. Therapies such as Homeopathy have become popular alternatives to the most modern treatments. Organic foods, grown naturally, are valued more than foods produced by sophisticated artificial methods. But now let's look forward . . .

The Soapburger Empire

Here's how Joseph P. Soapenburger III, international business tycoon, uses computers in his end-of-the-century competitive, white-hot financial world.

- He sends letters which he has written on a Wordprocessor containing programs that will check his spelling and grammar, and even supply him with a word if he's stuck for one (which is just as well, as Joseph got a U at GCSE English).

- Or, if he prefers, he can send documents from one computer to another (E mail) without bothering the Post Office at all.

- He stores all kinds of information on a database.

- Spreadsheets and accountancy applications keep an eye on all his financial wheeler-dealings.

- His publicity campaigns are set up using a Desk-Top-Publishing (DTP) application. TV commercials are edited on a computer, as is the music that goes with them.

- In Joseph's headquarters, computers control the heating and air conditioning.

- The people who design his products use Computer-Aided Design (CAD) programs.

- If Joseph or any of his employees need to find information, they use a variety of CD ROM discs including encyclopedias and atlases; or they surf the INTERNET to get information from all over the world (if they know where they need to look).

- If Joseph doesn't fancy a business trip, he arranges for a video-conference via computer, so that he can talk to other tycoons on a TV screen, and they can examine videotapes, documents and other information together.

- And when Joseph wants to relax, he goes to his private Virtual Reality suite, becomes Captain Zap, Space Ranger, and wipes out the Galactic Hordes.

COMPUTERS ARE IT

Computers were only born in the 1940s, but are already in to their fifth generation.

You name it at the end of the century, and computers are used to control it: air traffic, machinery, industrial processes, car engines, the central heating in your school ... (which might explain why it's always off when the weather is cold and on when it's warm). Modern computers can talk to each other along telephone lines (via a device called a Modem) and connect to a worldwide network of information (the INTERNET).

Joe and Josephine have barely started to explore the potential of the INTERNET. With it, they can access information from anywhere in the world. In future they will be able to use it to find out everything that's going on in the world, deal with their bank, do their shopping ... And their kids will be able to call up a learning package on it instead of going to school.

We bet that, in the 21st century, life will be just as exciting, confusing, terrible and hopeful as it has been made in the 20th by our greatest enemy ...

Ourselves!

TIMELINE

	1900-10	1911-20
Main Events	Boer War 1899-1902 Russo-Japanese War 1904-05	World War 1 1914-18 Russian Revolution 1917
British Monarch	Victoria 1837-1901 Edward VII 1901-10	George V 1910-36
Achievements	Wright brothers' flight 1903 Peary reaches N. Pole 1909 Blériot flies across Channel 1909	Amundsen reaches S. Pole 1911 Alcock and Brown fly across Atlantic 1919
Discoveries & Inventions	Hearing aids 1901 Four blood groups 1900 First successful blood transfusion 1905 Vitamins 1910	Poison gas, first used 1915 Tanks, first used 1916 Neurosurgery 1918 Rutherford splits atom 1919
Disasters	San Francisco earthquake 1906 (700 dead) Mont Pelée volcano, Martinique 1902 (30,000 dead)	*Titanic* hits iceberg 1912 (1,503 dead) German airship LZ-18 crashes 1913 (28 dead) German sub sinks *Lusitania* 1915 (1,400 dead)
Communications	First coded telegraph message across Atlantic 1901 First transmission by human voice 1906	Dame Nellie Melba recital broadcast from Chelmsford and heard throughout Europe 1915

1920s

Mussolini takes power in Italy 1922
Wall Street Crash 1929

George V 1910-36

First zeppelin flight across Atlantic 1924
Lindbergh flies solo New York to Paris 1927

Insulin 1921
Electron microscope 1926
Fleming discovers penicillin 1928
Iron lung 1929

Famine in USSR 1920-21 (5 million dead)
Tokyo earthquake 1923 (143,000 dead)

BBC radio broadcasts begin 1922
Logie Baird demonstrates television 1926

1930s

Hitler is Führer, Germany 1934/Spanish Civil War 1936-39/WW 2 begins

George V 1910-36
Edward VIII (abdicates)
George VI 1936-52

Eyston reaches 502 km/h in his car *Thunderbolt* 1937

Scotch tape 1930
Cat's eyes 1933
Antihistamine 1937
Helicopter 1939

Crash of British airship R101 1930 (48 dead)
Crash of German airship *Hindenburg* 1937 (34 dead)
Famine in USSR 1932-34 (5 million dead)

TV transmissions begin in Germany 1935
BBC TV begins 1936
First TV games shows 1938

1940s

World War 2 1939-45
Indian independence 1947
Creation of Israel 1948

George VI 1936-52

Heyerdahl sails balsa raft *Kon-tiki* from Peru to South Pacific 1947
Piccard explores ocean depths off West Africa, in bathyscaphe 1948

Aerosol spray 1941
Nuclear power station 1942
Aqualung 1943
Electronic computers, Colossus 1943 and ENIAC 1946
Fluoride 1945

Coal dust explosion, Benxihu colliery, China 1942 (1,550 dead)
Train crash, Salerno, Italy 1944 (526 dead)
Wilhelm Gustloff torpedoed by Russian sub 1945

Radar experts during the war become TV technicians afterwards

	1950s	**1960s**
Main Events	Korean War 1950-53 Vietnam War 1954-75 EEC founded 1957	Cuban missile crisis 1962 Assassination of J.F. Kennedy 1963
British Monarch	George VI 1936-52 Elizabeth II 1952-	Elizabeth II 1952-
Achievements	Hillary and Tenzing reach summit of Everest 1953	Gagarin, first man in space, orbits Earth in *Vostok* spaceship 1961 *Apollo* lands first men on Moon 1969
Discoveries & Inventions	Polio vaccine 1953 DNA 1953 Nuclear submarine 1954 Hormones 1956 Laser beams 1958 Hovercraft 1959	Industrial robots 1962 Human heart transplant 1967 Silicon microprocessor 1969
Disasters	Minamata mercury leak, Japan 1953	Aberfan landslip 1966 (144 dead) *Torrey Canyon* oil tanker spillage 1967 Famine in Nigeria 1967 (1 million dead)
Communications	Coronation of Elizabeth II televised worldwide 1953 First telephone cable between USA and Europe 1956	*Telstar* communications satellite launched 1962 Colour TV introduced in Britain 1967

1970s

Escalation of Irish "Troubles"
OPEC oil price rise 1973
End of Vietnam War 1975

Elizabeth II 1952-

Concorde flies at twice the speed of sound 1970
First woman (Junko Tabei of Japan) climbs Everest 1975

Nuclear magnetic resonance imaging 1973
First test-tube baby born 1978
Compact discs 1978

Famine in Sahel desert 1969-74 (1 million dead)
Nuclear reactor meltdown, Three Mile Island, USA 1979

Teletext first used 1974
Optic fibre cables developed for use in telecommunications 1976

1980s

Iran-Iraq War 1980-88
Falklands War 1982
E. and W. Germany reunited 1989

Elizabeth II 1952-

Italian Messener climbs Everest solo 1980
R. Swan first to walk to both S. Pole 1986 and N. Pole 1989

Compact disc player 1981
Launch of first space shuttle 1981
Artificial skin 1986

Chemical factory leak, Bhopal, India 1984 (3,350 dead)/Famine in Ethiopia 1984-85 (5 million dead)
Explosion of nuclear reactor, Chernobyl 1986

Sky satellite television begins broadcasting 1989

1990s

Collapse of USSR 1991
Gulf War 1991/War in Bosnia/Black government in power in South Africa

Elizabeth II 1952-

Norwegian Kagge first to reach S. Pole alone 1993

Virtual Reality games 1992
Robot milking machine 1993
Super-atom created 1995

Estonia ferry sinks in Baltic 1994 (900 dead)
Kobe earthquake, Japan 1995 (5,000 dead)
Sea Empress oil tanker spillage 1996

First electronic newspaper 1993
Channel Tunnel opened 1994
Interactive TV 1994

QUIZ ANSWERS

ANSWERS TO QUIZ ON PAGE 6

1. Paper clip
2. Safety razor
3. Vacuum cleaner
4. Production line
5. Electric toaster
6. Crystal radio
7. Autopilot
8. Photocopier
9. Frozen food

ANSWERS TO QUIZ ON PAGE 54

1. Insulin
2. Portable radio
3. Electron microscope
4. Tape recorder
5. Penicillin
6. Cat's eyes
7. Shopping trolleys
8. Biro
9. Nylon stockings
10. Helicopter

ANSWERS TO QUIZ ON PAGES 100–101

1. The first electronic computer (Electronic Numerical Integrator And Calculator)
2. Nuclear power station
3. Zebra crossing
4. Silicon chips
5. The hovercraft
6. Laser beam
7. Compact audiocassette
8. Telstar, the first communication satellite
9. Pocket calculator
10. Jumbo jet
11. Video recorder
12. TGV, French high-speed train
13. Walkman (personal stereo)
14. Compact disc (CD)

INDEX

abdication 53
Aberfan 93
African states 77
Africa, South 8, 10, 71, 72, 77, 79-80
Afrikaners 8, 79
AIDS 115
aircraft 14, 16, 25, 26, 27, 41, 53, 60
Albania 57, 82
Alcock, John 41
Aldrin, Buzz 91
Amiens, Battle of 28
Amin, Idi 78
Amritsar 74
Amundsen, Roald 15, 16
Apartheid 10, 79-80
appeasement 56
Arafat, Yasser 104
Armstrong, Neil 91
assassinations 18, 19, 35, 43, 76, 93, 98
Atlantic, Battle of the 60
Australia 71, 105
Ayatollah Khomeini 105

Baden-Powell, R. 9
Bangladesh 76, 105
Belgium 59, 82, 105, 113
Berlin Wall 82, 112
Biafra 78
Birdseye, Clarence 6
birth control pill 95
Blériot, Louis 16
Blitz 60, 63, 66, 69
Boer War 8-10, 73, 79
Bolsheviks 36, 38, 39, 40, 52
bombs 66-68, 83 (see also nuclear weapons)
Bosnia 110-111
Boxer Uprising 32, 33
Brando, Marlon 94
Braun, Eva 62
Britain, Battle of 60
Brown, Arthur 41
Bulgaria 82

Canada 71, 82, 105
Capitalism 42, 81
Capone, Al 45

cars 4, 41, 47, 117
Castro, Fidel 86
Chiang Kai-shek 50, 51
China 33, 50-51, 62, 83, 84-85
Churchill, Winston 59
cinema 41, 93, 94
Cod War 106
Cold War 70, 81-90
colonies 7, 11, 24, 29, 71, 77, 78
Commonwealth 71, 77
Communism 41, 42, 50, 51, 52, 81, 83, 84, 85, 87, 112
Communist Party (China) 50, 51
Communist Party (Russia) 36, 50, 52
computers 118-119
concentration camps 10, 48, 49
Cook, Frederick A. 13, 15
Cousteau, Jacques 91
Cuba 86
Cultural Revolution 85
Czars 11, 34, 35, 36,

125

37, 38, 39
Czechoslovakia 29, 57, 82, 105, 112

D-Day 62
Davison, Emily 31
Dean, James 94
Denmark 59, 82, 105, 113
depression 44-46, 52
Dominions 71, 79
Duma 36, 38
Dunkirk 59

Edward VIII 53
Eisenhower, General 61
El Alamein, Battle of 61
Elizabeth II 69, 93
Empire, British 7
energy 117
Engels, Friedrich 42
environment 116-117
Ethiopia 43, 57
European Union 113-114
evacuation 69
Everest 91
explorers 13, 15, 16, 91

Fascism 42, 43, 46, 50, 55, 57
Fleming, Alexander 54
Ford, Henry 6
France 56, 82, 105, 113
Franco, General 57

Gagarin, Yuri 91
Gallipoli 23
Gandhi, Mohandas 72, 73, 74, 75, 76, 79, 98
Gaulle, General de 114
George V 39, 75
George VI 53
Germany 19, 28, 29, 46, 55, 56, 57, 70, 82, 112, 113
Gillette 6
gold 7, 8
Gorbachev, Mikhail 111, 112
Greece 23, 82, 105, 113
guerilla warfare 10, 77, 87
Gulf War 104, 105-106

health 92, 115
hearing aid 4
Hess, Rudolf 47
Hillary, Edmund 91
Hindenburg airship 53

Hirohito, Emperor 55
Hiroshima 62, 68
Hitler 10, 46, 47, 48, 55, 56, 57, 59, 60, 62
Holocaust 48-49
Hungary 29, 82, 105, 112
Hussein, Sadam 104, 105, 106

Iceland 82
India 71, 72-76
Iran 105
Iraq 105
Ireland 107-109, 113
Iron Curtain 81
Israel 99, 102-104
Italy 42, 55, 56, 57, 61, 82, 105, 113

Japan 11, 12, 24, 50, 51, 55, 56, 61, 62, 68, 70, 96-97
Jinnah, Muhammad Ali 76
Jutland, Battle of 24

Kagge, Erling 16
Kashmir 76
Kennedy, John F. 86,

87, 93, 98
Kenya 78
Kenyatta, Jomo 78
Khrushchev, N. 86
Kimberley 8, 9
King, Martin Luther 73, 93, 98
Korea 11-12, 83
Kuomintang 50

Ladysmith 8, 9
Lawrence of Arabia 24
League of Nations 29, 56
Lebanon 104
Lenin, Vladimir I. 36, 39, 52
Lindbergh, Charles 41
Lusitania 25
Luxembourg 59, 82, 113

Macmillan, Harold 77
Mafeking 8, 9
Maginot Line 56, 59
Manchuria 11, 50
Mandela, Nelson 80
Mao Tse-tung 50, 51, 84, 85
Marne, Battle of the 22
Marx, Karl 42
Mau Mau 78

May the Fourth Movement 50
McCarthy, Joe 86
Midway, Battle of 61
Montgomery, General 61
moon 91
Mussolini 42, 43, 55, 57, 61

Nagasaki 62, 68
National Health Service 92
NATO 82, 111
Nazi (National Socialist Workers) Party 46
Nazism 47, 48, 55, 62, 103, 108
Nehru, Jawaharlal 72, 76
Netherlands 59, 82, 105, 113
New Deal 45
New Zealand 71, 105
Nigeria 78
Nixon, President 88, 89
Norgay, Tenzing 91
Norway 59, 82, 105
nuclear power 117
nuclear weapons 68, 83, 84, 86, 90
Oates, Titus 16

Obote, Milton 78
OPEC 99
Operation Overlord 62

Pakistan 76, 105
Palestine 102-104
Pankhurst, Emmeline 30
Pearl Harbor 12, 61
Peary, Robert 15
Piccard, Auguste and Jacques 91
Poland 49, 57, 82, 105, 112
Poles
 North 13, 15
 South 15, 16
Portugal 82, 113
Potemkin 12, 35
Prohibition 45

R101 airship 53
radio 41, 53
Rasputin, Grigori Y. 37-38
rationing 63, 64, 91
Rhodesia 79
Richthofen, Manfred von 27
Romania 82, 112
Rommel, General 61

Roosevelt, Franklin D. 45
Russia 11, 12, 32, 34, 36, 37, 40 (*see also* USSR)
Russian Revolution 12, 28, 32, 34-36, 38-39
Russo-Japanese War 11

Scott, Robert F. 15, 16
Shintoism 55
Siberia 36
Sikorsky, Igor 54
Simpson, Wallis 53
Soccer War 109
Solidarity 112
Somme, Battle of the 22
space 91
Spain 82, 105, 113
Spanish Civil War 57
Spion Kop, Battle of 8
Sputnik 91
Stalin, Josef 40, 52, 57, 60, 84
Stalingrad, Battle of 60
strikes 32, 35, 36, 38, 44
  General Strike, 1926 44
submarines 24, 25, 60
Suez 103

suffragettes 30, 31
Sun Yat-sen 50

tanks 28, 29
teenagers 94
television 89, 93, 94
Tito 110
Togo, Admiral 12
Toscanini, Arturo 43
trench warfare 21, 22
Trotsky, Leon 36, 40
Tsushima, Battle of 12, 34
Turkey 23, 24, 82, 102

U-boats 60
Uganda 78
United Nations 70, 103, 105
USA 11, 25, 45, 56, 61, 62, 70, 81, 82, 83, 86, 87, 90, 94, 103, 105, 106
USSR 40, 49, 52, 56, 57, 60, 70, 81, 82, 83, 84, 90, 105, 107, 110, 111, 112

Verdun, Battle of 22

Vereeniging, Peace of 10
Vietnam War 10, 87-79
Volkswagen 47

Wall Street crash 45
Warsaw Pact 82
Watergate scandal 89
women 30, 31, 70, 95
World War 1 17-29, 31, 41, 46, 70, 102
World War 2 41, 45, 48, 49, 55-70, 71, 75, 77, 82, 94, 95, 96, 108
Wright, Orville and Wilbur 14

Yugoslavia 29, 110
Ypres, Battle of 22, 28

zeppelins 27, 53